SUSTAINABLE PRACTICES IN BUSINESS - A PARADIGM SHIFT

DR. DHANYA K A & JASEENA K B

RIGI PUBLICATION

SUSTAINABLE PRACTICES IN BUSINESS - A PARADIGM SHIFT

BY

DR. DHANYA K A & JASEENA K B

Originally published in India

ISBN: 978-93-95773-32-4

Published by RIGI PUBLICATION

777, Street no.9, Krishna Nagar

Khanna-141401 (Punjab), India

Website: www.rigipublication.com

Email: info@rigipublication.com

Phone: +91-9357710014, +91-9465468291

LIST OF CONTENTS

INFLUENCE OF BEHAVIOURAL FINANCE ON THE STOCK MARKET INVESTMENT DECISIONS OF INDIVIDUALS: A STUDY WITH SPECIAL REFERENCE TO MALABAR REGION OF KERALA

ATHIRA KT

Research Scholar, Kaamadhenu Arts and Science College, Bharathiyar University, Coimbatore

ABSTRACT

Investment is an inevitable element of every individual lives. Depending upon the purpose andother financial constraints, one has to select the most appropriate investment opportunity for better results in future. After so many advancements in the national as well as international economy, varied forms of investment avenues are available. The most popular and vibrant among them is the stock market investment. But the selection of an optimal portfolio is subjectto a number of factors such as objectives, financial background, market analysis, rationality, behavioral factors, changes in economy, govt interventions etc. As per the literature review it was found that today's investors and their actions are different from that of the traditional investors. Behavioral factors exhibit a prominent effect. So, the present study is aimed at finding the influence of behavioral finance on the stock market investment decisions of individuals. It also covers the effect of demographic features on decision making and the relation between risk bearing capabilities and behavioral factors. The paper is based on primarydata which was collected through a well-structured questionnaire and circulated as google form among 125 respondents especially in the Malabar region of Kerala. The sample was selected through purposive as well as snowball sampling technique. Important psychological biases such as heuristic, prospect and herding factors were considered for study. Statistical tools suchas correlation, chi-square, independent sample t-test, one-way anova and factor analysis were used for analysis.

Key words: investment, behav1ioral finance, heuristic factors, prospect factors, herding effect,risk bearing capabilities

INTRODUCTION

As human beings, expectations about future drives our lives. In order to bring our dreams into practice, everyone must be well equipped with sufficient financial resources. So, financial planning and decision making is the most vital element of human lives. Financial planning is the process of meeting financial goals through the proper management of finances.Based on the economic status of individuals corresponding investments has to be made for a better future. Today, varieties of investment avenues are available such as savings bank accounts, post office savings, mutual fund, stock market, real estates, gold etc. Nowadays, majority of people are engaged in stock market investments. Based on a number of factors suchas purpose, period, risk, return, liquidity, regulations, tax burden etc. one has to make the mostappropriate portfolio to ensure a well satisfied return on time. Proper research and planning arerequired to avoid unwise decisions which may eventually lead to unfavorable results.

In contrary to long held traditional theories of finance, people are not always rational and markets are not always efficient. That means, People in standard finance are rational. People in behavioural finance are normal (Statman). There arises the importance of BehavioralFinance which is a subfield of Behavioral Economics. Fundamentally, behavioural finance is about understanding how people make decisions, both individually and collectively. Byunderstanding how investors and markets behave, it may be possible to modify or adapt to these behaviours in order to improve economic outcomes. In many instances, knowledge of and integration of behavioural finance may lead to superior results for both advisors and their clients (Pompian). It explores how factors like psychological influences and biases distort the logical reasoning of people. Behavioral Finance can be defined as "a relatively new field that seeks to combine behavioral and cognitive psychological theory with conventional economicsand finance to provide explanations for why people make irrational financial decisions (Tversky). Nobel Prize winner Daniel Kahneman is one of the founding fathers of BehavioralFinance.

On this ground, it is very essential to have a proper knowledge and use of Behavioral Finance. Because, based on the insights from psychology, it depicts how human behavior andbiases influences the decisions of individuals.

CONVENTIONAL FINANCE

The foundations of modern finance are based on rational decision making which is called Conventional Finance. The rational behaviour helps in avoiding uncertainty about the future. The individuals maximize utility (or happiness) based on their preferences, the constraints they face, and the information at their disposal. There is abundant evidence that most people avoid risk in most circumstances. However, they are willing to assume risk if theyare compensated for it (Lucy F. Ackert). So, under this concept people have rational preferences across possible outcomes or states of nature, they maximize utility and make independent decisions based on all relevant information. Under this area of study there is no role for psychological factors in individual decision making.

BEHAVIOURAL FINANCE

Behavioural finance is commonly defined as 'the application of psychology to finance'(Pompian, Behavioral Finance and Investor Types, 2012). It covers the phenomena ranging from individual investors to market level outcomes. Standard finance or conventional finance is basically built on rules about how investors should behave, rather than on principles describing how they actually behave. On the other hand, Behavioural finance attempts to identify and learn from the human psychological phenomena at work in financial markets andwithin individual investors. Like standard finance, behavioural finance is ultimately governedby basic precepts and assumptions. However, standard finance grounds its assumptions in idealized financial behaviour where behavioural finance grounds its assumptions in observed financial behaviour. Behavioural finance helps to understand how financial decisions are greatly influenced by human emotion, biases, and cognitive limitations of the mind in processing and responding to information. It explains why the individual decisions are alwaysmight not appear to be rational and how the psychological factors affect the decision making of individual investors as well as the financial markets.

HEURISTIC FACTORS

Heuristics is a subfield of cognitive psychology and behavioural science. They are shortcuts tosimplify the assessment of probabilities in decision making. Heuristic is a decision rule that utilizes a subset of the information set.

Anchoring

Anchoring bias occurs when people rely too much on pre-existing information or the first information they find while making decisions. It happens regardless of accuracy of information. This anchoring information can be used as a point of reference when the initial data matches our beliefs or expectations, investors disregard any subsequent information that challenges it.

Availability/Recency Bias

Due to this bias, investors believe that the facts most relevant to their own lives are most relevant to the success of an investment. When one has such a bias, possibilities that we can easily recall and most familiar with seem more likely to be true than those that are less familiar. (Pompian, Behavioral Finance and Investor Types, 2012). In this case, the biased people incorrectly believe that recent events will occur again soon, which is irrational.

Representation Bias

This bias is strongly rooted in our desire to have the information we need to process fit into a neat framework.

It helps to quickly absorb new information but, it also allows us to perceive those probabilities that fit into the framework of what we want to perceive. (Pompian,Behavioral Finance and Investor Types, 2012). For example, if someone believes that good companies make good investments, it is a type of representation bias.

Overconfidence

Overconfidence is best described as the unwarranted faith in one's own thoughts and abilities.There exists the investors' overestimation of the knowledge, abilities and quality of their judgment. Many aggressive investors believe that they have an above-average aptitude for selecting investments.

PROSPECT FACTORS

The basic concept behind prospect theory is that the investors value losses and gains differentlywhile making decisions.

Prospect Bias

Prospect theory is positive or descriptive because it is firmly based on how people actually behave. It opines that, investor's value gains and losses differently, placing more weight on perceived gains than perceived losses. An investor presented with a choice, both equal, will choose the one presented in terms of potential gains.

Loss Aversion

An investor having loss aversion bias tend to feel the pain of losses more acutely than the pleasure of gaining. There are two key contexts in which loss aversion can be seen. Some investors may invest in any single stock. Shortly after the investment, if the stock value drops, they may hold on to the same, feeling painful to take the loss. Likewise, some may invest in adiversified basket of asset classes. During market meltdowns loss aversion behaviour can be seen which is wealth destructing.

Mental Accounting

According to Richard Thaler, "mental accounting is the set of cognitive operations used byindividuals and households to organize, evaluate, and keep track of financial activities." (Lucy F. Ackert). It is the tendency to treat the same money differently depending on where it camefrom or what we intend to do with it. In this case, the full scope of the finance is ignored.

Regret Aversion

Regret aversion describes a negative emotional bias that urges the investors to avoid regret, thus sometimes making wrong decision. For example, if an investor fears the consequences ofboth not buying the right investment property and buying the wrong investment property, the person is likely to be subject to the bias of regret aversion.

HERDING FACTORS

The herding behavior happens when people join in groups and follow the actions of others without considering their own opinions and analysis. Their self-judgement stops at this point and follows the group actions accordingly.

METHODOLOGY

The study is of a quantitative nature. The sample consists of 125 respondents from the Malabarregion of Kerala, who were identified using purposive as well as snowball sampling methods.A well-structured questionnaire was administered as google form to collect the data. It was then analysed using statistical tools such as chi-square, independent sample t-test, correlation,one-way anova and factor analysis, with the help of SPSS.

OBJECTIVES

1. To study various investment avenues and their preferences in stock market domain
2. To analyze the effect of demographic features on the individual's behavioral factors
3. To study the influence of behavioral factors on the investment decisions
4. To know the relationship between risk bearing capabilities and behavioral factors

ANALYSIS

Table 1: Preferences of investment avenues

Financial assets	Percentage
Shares	95
Debentures	12
Bonds	11
Mutual Funds	65

The respondents under study make their investments in shares, debentures, bonds and mutual funds. It was clear from the table that most of the respondents (95%) prefer to invest in shares,followed by mutual funds (65%). Only a few of the respondents choose Bonds and debenturesfor the purpose of investment in the stock market.

Table 2: Relation between gender and behavioural factors

Gender	Mean	SD	T value	P value
Male	2.4427	1.27584	-1.627	.113
Female	3.3962	3.17953		

H0: The means of the two groups are not significantly different

The test result shows t-statistic of -1.627. The corresponding p value is .113, which is greaterthan 0.05. Therefore, we can accept the null hypothesis that the means of male and female arenot significantly different. And it can be concluded that both male and female investors are equally influenced by the behavioral factors.

Table 3 : Relation between age and behavioural factors

		Age	Behavioural Factors
Age	Pearson Correlation	1	.004
	Sig. (2-tailed)		.968
	N	125	125
Behavioural Factors	Pearson Correlation	.004	1
	Sig. (2-tailed)	.968	
	N	125	125

H0: there is no correlation between age and behavioural factors

We can see that the Pearson Correlation Co-efficient is .004. this is not statistically significantsince the p value is greater than .05 i.e.,968. So, we can accept the null hypothesis and can be concluded that there is no relation between age and behavioural factors.

Table 4: Educational Qualification and behavioral factors

Educational qualification	Mean	SD	F value	P value
Up to 10th	2.2000	.80139	.521	.720
Plus two	3.4037	3.01445		
UG	2.7938	2.13950		
PG	2.5491	1.81618		
Above PG	2.3242	.33635		

H0: There is no significant difference in the behavioural factors with regard to the educationalqualification of investors

The p value is found to be .720 which is above .05. So, there is no significant difference in theeffect of behavioural factors with regard to the education levels of investors.

Table 5: Marital status and behavioural factors

Marital status	Mean	Sd	T value	P value
Married	2.2988	.39616	-1.987	.054
Unmarried	3.2366	3.00911		

H0: The means of the two groups are not significantly different

The test result shows t-statistic of -1.987. The corresponding p value is .054, which is greaterthan 0.05. Therefore, we can accept the null hypothesis that the means of married and unmarried investors are not significantly different and are equally influenced by the behavioralfactors.

Table 6: Type of Employment and Behavioral factors

Type of employment	Mean	SD	F value	P value
Student	2.3521	.31300	.382	.860
Self-employed	2.6873	1.99711		
Private employee	2.7652	2.14791		
Govt. employee	2.2927	.38422		
Semi-govt. employee	2.1667	.26891		
Retired	2.0917	.45755		

H0: There is no significant difference in the behavioural factors with regard to the type of employment of the investors

The p value is found to be .860 which is above .05. So, the null hypothesis is accepted and canbe concluded that there is no significant difference in the effect of behavioural factors with regard to various types of employment in which the investors are engaged.

Table 7: Annual income and behavioral factors

Annual income	Mean	SD	F value	P value
Below 2 Lakhs	3.1068	2.84481	1.202	.312
2-4 Lakhs	2.6303	1.43865		
4-6 Lakhs	2.6319	1.95482		
Above 6 Lakhs	2.2133	.38298		

H0: There is no significant difference in the bf with regard to the annual income of the investors

The p value is found to be .312 which is above .05. So, the null hypothesis is accepted and canbe concluded that there is no significant difference in the effect of behavioural factors with regard to the annual income of the investors.

Table 8: Relationship between investment experience and behavioural factors

		EXPERIENCE	BEHAVIOURAL BIAS
EXPERIENCE	Pearson Correlation	1	.388*
	Sig. (2-tailed)		.000
	N	125	125
BEHAVIOURAL BIAS	Pearson Correlation	.388*	1
	Sig. (2-tailed)	.000	
	N	125	125

H0: there is no correlation between experience in investing and behavioural factors

We can see that the Pearson Correlation Co-efficient is .388. This is statistically significant since the p value is less than .05. So, we can reject the null hypothesis and can be concluded that there is a relation between experience and behavioural factors. But the correlation is foundto be low.

Table 9: Period of investment and behavioural factors

Period of investment	Mean	SD	F value	P value
Less than one year	2.2408	.38789	3.804	.025
1-3 Years	2.6851	1.61965		
More than 3 Years	3.3439	3.14469		

H0: There is no significant difference in the bf with regard to the period of investment

The p value is found to be .025 which is below .05. So, there is a significant difference in the effect of behavioural factors with regard to various periods for which investment is made by the investors.

Table 10: Relation between how investors make decisions and behavioural factors

		Investment decision	Behavioural Factors
Investment decision	Pearson Correlation	1	-.044
	Sig. (2-tailed)		.624
	N	125	125
Behavioural factors	Pearson Correlation	-.044	1
	Sig. (2-tailed)	.624	
	N	125	125

H0: there is no correlation between the mode of decision making and behavioural factors

We can see that the Pearson Correlation Co-efficient is -.044. This is statistically not significantsince the p value is greater than .05. So, we can accept the null hypothesis and can be concludedthat there is a negative correlation between how investors take decisions and behavioural factors.

Table11: Satisfaction on existing portfolio and behavioural factors

Satisfaction on existing portfolio	Mean	SD	T value	P value
Yes	2.3139	.42499	-1.596	.119
No	2.9447	2.41917		

H0: The means of the two groups are not significantly different

The test result shows t-statistic of -1.596. The corresponding p value is .119, which is greaterthan 0.05. Therefore, we can accept the null hypothesis that the means of investors who are satisfied and not satisfied with the existing portfolio are not significantly different. And it canbe concluded that both satisfied and non-satisfied investors are equally influenced by the behavioral factors.

Table12: Gender and satisfaction on existing portfolio

	Satisfaction on existing portfolio		**Total**	**Chi Square**	**P Value**
	YES	NO			
Male	64	30	94	.001	.972
Female	21	10	31		

H0: there is no association between gender and satisfaction on existing portfolio

Here the x^2 value is .001 and p value is .972. Hence the p value is more than the significance level i.e., .05. So, we accept the null hypothesis that there is no association between gender andsatisfaction on existing portfolio.

Table 13: Risk tolerance level and behavioural factors

Risk tolerance level	**Mean**	**SD**	**F value**	**P value**
High	2.3038	.49377	11.803	.000
Medium	2.3841	1.03551		
Low	4.6578	4.34777		

H0: There is no significant difference in the effect of bf with regard to the risk tolerance levelof the investors

The p value is found to be .000 which is below .05. So, there is a significant difference in the effect of behavioural factors with regard to the risk tolerance level of the investors.

Table 14: factor analysis to find out the most influenced behavioural factor

Factor analysis is conducted to know the most influenced behavioural factor for the investors while making investment in the stock market. KMO is calculated to find out the sample adequacy.

KMO and Bartlett's Test

Kaiser-Meyer-Olkin Measure of Sampling Adequacy.		.682
Bartlett's Test of Sphericity	Approx. Chi-Square	168.054
	Df	45
	Sig.	.000

The test revealed 0.682 of KMO sampling adequacy, which is greater than 0.6 and the Bartlett's Test of Sphericity is significant. The test leads to the conclusion that the data set is appropriatefor Factor Analysis (EFA).

Communalities

	Initial	Extraction
ANCHORING BIAS	1.000	.518
AVAILABILITY BIAS	1.000	.577
REPRESENTATION BIAS	1.000	.749
OVER CONFIDENCE	1.000	.687
PROSPECT FACTORS	1.000	.547
LOSS AVERSION	1.000	.538
MENTAL ACCOUNTING 1	1.000	.442
MENTAL ACCOUNTING 2	1.000	.662
REGRET AVERSION	1.000	.743
HERDING EFFECT	1.000	.744

Extraction Method: Principal Component Analysis.

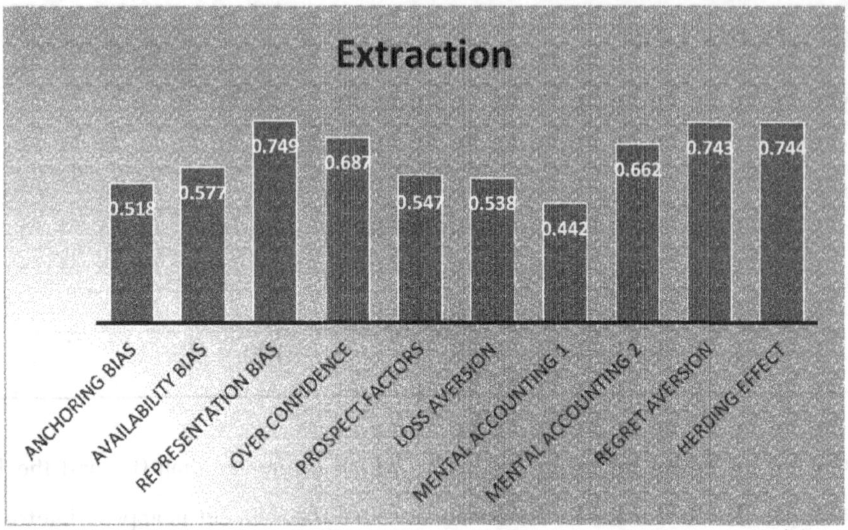

It is clear from the figure that representation bias, herding effect and regret aversion are the most influenced behavioural biases for the investors while making investment decisions in thestock market.

DISCUSSIONS

- For analysis purpose, the behavioural factors were classified as heuristics, prospects and herding factors. The results of the study shows that representation bias, herding effect and regret aversion are the most influenced behavioural biases for the investors under consideration, while making investment decisions in the stock market. It was found that majority of the respondents prefer to invest in shares (95%), followed by mutual fund (65%)
- The study clearly depicts the fact that there is no effect of demographic features on the behavioural bias of individuals. For this purpose, demographic features such as gender, age,educational qualification, marital status, type of employment, and annual income were compared with the behavioural factors. And all the null hypothesis were accepted with p values .113,.968,.720,.054,.860, and .312 respectively.
- The analysis also throws lights on the relation between the effect of behavioural bias on theinvestment decisions of the respondents. The findings include, there is no relation that howinvestors make decisions, and in between satisfied and non-satisfied investors on their existing portfolio, with regard to the behavioural factors. And there is a significant difference in the effect of behavioural factors with regard to various periods for which investment is made. But, based on the year of experience in stock market investment, behavioural bias may vary from investor to investor.
- As per the analysis, it was understood that, there is no association between gender of the respondents and their satisfaction with the existing portfolio. And there is a significant difference in the effect of behavioural factors with regard to the risk tolerance level of the investors.

CONCLUSION

Successful financial decision making is one of the herculean tasks for every individual is concerned, which will be contributing to better tomorrow. There is a saying that "the trendis your friend" which means according to the trends in the market our choices may vary. Personality characteristics and behavioural biases forms an integral part of investment decision making especially in the domain of stock market. To study the influence of such psychological factors in the individual's decision making, heuristic factors such as anchoring bias, representative/recency bias, representative bias, and over-confidence; prospect factors like prospect bias, loss aversion, mental accounting and regret aversion; along with herding bias were considered and analysed. And it can be concluded that, there is no effect of demographic features on the behavioural factors of the investors. Even though the investor decision making is influenced by the psychological biases the most reflective among them includes representation bias, herding effect and regret aversion. Thus, it is advised to have a control over the emotional factors while taking stock market investment decision to cope up with this dynamic environment as well as to ensure a successful and strong financial ground in future.

REFERENCES

Choudhari, A. K. (2013). Impact of behavioral finance in investment decisions and strategies- A fresh approach. *IJMRBS*.

Daniel Kahneman, T. G. (2002). *Heuristics and Biases- The Psychology of Intuitive Judgement.* The Press Syndicate of the University of Cambridge.

Lucy F. Ackert, R. D. (n.d.). *Behavioral Finance -Psychology, Decision Making and Markets.* South-Western Cengage Learning.

Muhammad Atif Sattar, M. T. (2020). Behavioral Finance Biases in Investment Decision Making.

International Journal of Accounting,Finance and Risk Management.

Pompian, M. M. (2012). *Behavioral Finance and Investor Types.* John Wiley and Sons.

Randall Peteros, J. M. (2013). Application of behavioral finance concepts to investment decision making:suggestions for improving investment education courses. *International journal ofmanagement.*

Raut, R. K. (2020). Past Behavior, Financial Literacy and investment decision making process of individual investors. *International Journal of Emerging Markets.*

5S-KAIZEN-TQM MODEL FOR QUALITY IMPROVEMENT IN HEALTHCARE ORGANIZATIONS

Ayisha K

Research scholar, Dept of commerce & management studies, PSMO College, Tirurangadi.

Dr. Ayoob CP

Research Supervisor, Dept of commerce &management studies, PSMO College, Tirurangadi.

Abstract

Healthcare has grown to be one of India's most important industries, both in terms of services and revenue. Hospitals, medical devices, clinical trials, outsourcing, telemedicine, medical tourism, health insurance, and medical equipment are all part of healthcare. The Indian healthcare system is expanding rapidly as a result of improved coverage, expanded services, and increased spending by both public and private entities. The stake holders of the healthcare industries are focusing to receiving the quality services with reasonable cost and that demands the authorities to continuous improvement in the overall quality of healthcare industry. The 5S-Kaizen-TQM Approach is one of the instruments for quality improvement in health care. 5S-Kaizen-TQM strategy is a three-step process for improving hospital administration with limited resources. This paper tends to give a framework about5S-Kaizen-TQM approach and its core benefits and need of implementing it in health care organizations in order to enrich the quality improvement in health sector. It will help the stakeholders for better control and management and systematic analysis of the industry.

Keywords: Total Quality Management, 5S-kaizen approach, 5S-kaizen-TQM approach, framework of healthcare quality improvisation. TQM implementation,

Introduction

According to the Economic Survey of 2022, India's public spending on healthcare in 2021-22 would be 2.1% of GDP, up from 1.8% in 2020-21 and 1.3% in 2019-20. The Indian healthcare industry is predicted to triple in size between 2016 and 2022, rising at a CAGR of 22% to reach US$ 372 billion in 2022, up from US$ 110 billion in 2016. Indian healthcare infrastructure is anticipated to be worth $349.1 billion by FY22.(*Indian Healthcare Industry Analysis | IBEF*, n.d.) Hospitals offer important services to individuals, despite the fact that stack holders have been reported to be dissatisfied with the services supplied by hospitals. This is the effect of failing to satisfy the consumers' expectations. Expectations might be healthcare-related or non-health-related, such as dignity, fundamental human needs, rapid attention in care and treatment, good communication, and so on. Proper control over the work method may significantly increase hospital effectiveness in terms of both services and revenues. Improving the quality and safety of health services is a key concern in low- and middle-income countries

(Harrison et al., 2015), where the actual amount of risky healthcare practices is unknown. Wilson observed that the rates of avoidable injury, unexpected expenditure and death are rising, prompting concern among policymakers and healthcare practitioners (Wilson et al., 2012; World Health Organization, 2012). In response, several quality improvement (QI) projects have emerged in low- and middle-income nations' health sectors to train healthcare personnel in various QI methodologies (Heiby, 2014; Aveling et al., 2015). Despite such efforts, quality and safety in healthcare remain key challenges (World Health Organization, 2016). QI techniques have transitioned from quality control (QC) or quality assurance to total quality management (TQM). This paradigm, which was introduced into the health care sector in the late 1990s, strives to enhance productivity and effectiveness by maximizing the use of health resources in order to deliver high quality medical services and patient safety. TQM activities currently are being implemented in many health care facilities in Asia, Europe and the USA (Chakravarty et al., 2001; Balasubramanian, 2016). The 5S-KAIZEN-TQM Approach is one of the instruments for quality improvement in health care. This strategy is based on Japanese management and was designed primarily for the industries. However, the basic principle is also applicable to the health-care industry. One of the main goals of 5S-KAIZEN is to remove waste in the workplace. 5S is a concept and method of arranging and controlling the work environment and work flow with the goal of increasing efficiency by eliminating waste, enhancing flow, and lowering process unreasonableness. 5S will discover and eliminate anomalies and wastes in processes. KAIZEN is a continual problem-solving process that uses current resources to enhance the working environment, processes, and circumstances. Kaizen may assist a hospital in developing a culture of continuous quality improvement in order to satisfy internal and external clients. Kaizen improves things incrementally and the goal. TQM (Total Quality Management) is a multidisciplinary and participative process that optimizes all categories of operations in all departments/units and personnel in order to provide high-quality services. TQM procedures (consisting of 5S and Kaizen) should be included into institutional management frameworks in order to achieve high productivity and service quality.

Objectives of the study

The 5s KAIZEN TQM is a relevant approach in service sector and manufacturing sector. The author focusing on some of the main objectives for the study. They are as follows

- To provide an insight to the basic concepts of 5S-KAIZEN-TQM Approach
- To understand what are the tools used in 5s KAIZEN TQM approach
- To understand benefits of 5S and KAIZEN-TQM activities
- To create a conceptual framework for the 5s KAIZEN-TQM approach

Introduction of the 5S-KAIZEN-TQM approach in the global health sector

Several countries, mainly the United States and European nations, have implemented the 5S and KAIZEN (lean management) approaches in their health-care systems. Many low- and middle-income nations in Asia, the Middle East, and Africa are making similar efforts. For example, in 2007, JICA launched the Asia-Africa Knowledge Co-Creation Program (AAKCP). A total of 15 African nations joined AAKCP to learn more about these Asian practices (Ishijima et al., 2014). So far, 29 low- and middle-income countries, including Bangladesh, Tanzania, and Uganda, have implemented the 5S-KAIZEN-TQM method in the health sector through government-initiated programs, resulting in improved hospital services (Ministry of Health, Labor and Welfare, Japan, 2018). Hospitals offer important services to individuals, despite the fact that stack holders grumble about the services given by hospitals. This is due to a failure to satisfy the consumers' expectations. The expectation may be healthcare-related or non-health-related, such as dignity, fundamental human needs, rapid attention in care and treatment, good communication, and so on. Non-fulfillment of expectations can occur as a result of active failures when rules and regulations are broken, or as a result of latent failures caused by design flaws, incorrectly constructed procedures, construction breakdowns, and so on. Controlling the work method properly may significantly increase the effectiveness of hospitals in terms of both services and income.

Introduction of the 5S-KAIZEN-TQM approach in the Indian health sector

Quality management necessitates a series of interconnected operations that ensure the quality of services in accordance with established standards and try to improve upon them by methodical planning, implementation, checking, and acting on compliances. The standards in this area are concerned with potential for improvement in order to increase service quality and patient happiness. These criteria are consistent with the facility-based quality assurance programme outlined in the 'Operational Guidelines'. The Indian health sector are continuously improvising their quality practices to better dispersion of services. National Quality Assurance Standards (2020) revised the quality standards and suggest the quality control practices like quality team and its periodic review, measurement of patients and employee satisfaction surveys, feedback analysis, preparing action plan and the implementation of internal quality assurance programmes inside departments, such as EQAS of diagnostic services, daily rounds and the use of departmental checklists, External Quality Assurance Service (EQAS) records at the laboratory, and so on. Interviews with Matron, Hospital Managers, Nurse In charges, OT Technicians, and others may reveal how they make daily rounds of departments and use checklists. The Use of quality tools and methodologies such as process mapping, control charts, the 5-'S', and so on. The examiner should look for any particular procedures and instruments used for quality improvement (Maqbool et al., 2013).

Background to the 5S-KAIZEN-TQM approach

Conceptually, Lean (Lean management) is an organisational culture based on management philosophy, principles, and methods that tries "to contribute to the sustainable development of society and the environment through the creation and provision of high-quality and innovative goods and services" (Toyota Code of Conduct., 2006). Lean produces a considerable boost in production efficiency and product quality. The lean management starts from continuous improvement work processes, purposes and people. Toyota implement it in its units and they achieved significant improvement in the productivity, efficiency and cycle time and cost efficiency.(Chiarini et al., 2018). Lean methodology relies on 3 simple ideas like deliver value, eliminate wastage, and continues improvement.(Chiarini et al., 2018). It has some tools to improve safety and quality like 5s methodology ,Muda, kaizen approach etc.it was used in manufacturing sector ,but recent years it has been using in other sectors also like service sector especially in healthcare(*5S-Kaizen-TQM Model for Quality Improvement of Healthcare Organization*, n.d.).TQM appears often in the health care sector with some literature emphasizing the strong relationship between the TQM and KAIZEN approaches (Saleem et al., 2012; Janjić et al., 2018; Rouf et al., 2017). Saleem et al. (2012) found that KAIZEN is a beneficial technique for attaining TQM through continuous improvement of process, quality, and performance, as well as human resource development. Many studies have also been conducted to improve hospital performance and service quality by implementing lean and KAIZEN concepts (Tortorella et al., 2016; Filho et al., 2015; Kanamori et al., 2016). KAIZEN is described as "constant improvement for greater quality, safety, and productivity through the work culture and collaboration of all employees" (Imai, 2012). The KAIZEN philosophy is founded on the notion that there is always opportunity for improvement in every process. Originally implemented in manufacturing, the KAIZEN idea is now often used in service industries such as office, aviation, hotel, and healthcare services (Saleem et al., 2012; Shan et al., 2016; Mazzocato et al., 2016). Kaizen is a continual problem-solving process that uses current resources to enhance the working environment, processes, and circumstances. Kaizen may assist a hospital in developing a culture of continuous quality improvement in order to satisfy internal and external clients. Kaizen improves things one step at a time, with the goal of "your work" as the end goal. Another component of this paradigm is the 5S method to workplace organisation, which is based on five Japanese words: seiri (sort), seiton (set), seisou (shine), seiketsu (standardise), and hitsuke (sustain). The 5S activity originated in Japan's manufacturing sectors, signifying a Japanese kind of quality control (Ishijima, 2016; MoHSW, Tanzania, 2013). The 5S method is a component of the KAIZEN method (Ishijima etal. 2014; Kanamori et al., 2016). 5S will identify the abnormalities and wastes in processes and reduce them.

What 5s can do?

It is a philosophy, way of organising managing workspace and work flows with an intension to improve efficiency by avoiding wastage improving flows and reducing process unreasonableness.

5S stands for Sort, Set, Shine, Standardise, Sustain. It is a step wise approach for better management and quality healthcare. It helps to

- Identify abnormalities: identify waste, reduce waste like over processing, over production, over inventory, waiting, motion, transportation, rework
- Promote to everyone for participation
- Improve safety
- Improve productivity (*5S-Kaizen-TQM Model for Quality Improvement of Healthcare Organization*, n.d.)

How kaizen approach benefited?

it is another component of 5s-kaizen -TQM approach which find root cause of problem and suggest solution with available facilities the main target of this approach is to reduce waste in work place and ensuring the maximum use of existing resources. It helps hospitals to create continuous quality improvement culture to meet external client satisfaction and expectations. This approach targets your work. The advantages of application of kaizen relies in the all-round improvement of hospital management. Improve the quality of services and strengthen the teamwork. KAIZEN can help a hospital to create "continuous quality improvement culture" to meet in/external clients' satisfaction and expectation

What kaizen can do?

- Find root cause of problems and solutions
- Improve all kind of hospital management
- Improve quality of services
- Strengthen teamwork

How TQM approach works?

It is a multidisciplinary and participatory approach with continuity by all categories of staff for realising high quality services. There are several TQM attributes which helps to performance evaluation of health care sector (Islam & Salam, 2022) such as

- Top leadership commitment
- Performance management system
- Continuous improvement
- Employee empowerment
- Effective operational management
- Patients' satisfaction etc.

All these integration results overall performance of hospital management. If there is any kind of deviations that can be identified and solute with an effective integrated system called 5s-kaizen-TQM approach.

What TQM can do?

- Improve quality of final products and services
- Increase customer satisfaction
- Visible growth of organisation
- Making right decision for quality improvement
- Reducing cost
- Managing whole facility with certain level of quality

Is 5s kaizen -TQM approach is effective for healthcare industry?

Traditionally, the greatest degree of medical treatment and diagnosis was required to ensure the quality of medical services. Unfortunately, despite high-level medical equipment in wealthy nations, numerous significant medical incidents happened in the 1990s, leading to widespread discontent with the care services given. We believed that employees were accountable and should not make mistakes.(Kanamori et al., 2016a) However, it is normal for humans to make mistakes, which is why it is critical to develop a system that decreases accidents. Furthermore, the quality-of-care services were restricted to clinical practise and did not take into account organisational issues such as waiting time to be served, time required to locate a document or equipment, and so on. As a result, the quality-of-healthcare service and medical safety definitions were revised. According to (Kanamori et al(2016), quality of healthcare services must involve quality management, which consists of providing what patients desire and is inherently crucial to patients. International trends in health and medical care quality are currently entering the fourth Medical Care Revolution, in which we are transitioning to process digitalization to improve operations and eliminate mistakes.(Hammami et al., 2022). In this context, in 2007, the Japan International Cooperation Agency (JICA) launched "Total Quality Management (TQM) for Better Hospital Services," a sub-program of the Asia-Africa Knowledge Co-creation Program (AAKCP) aimed at improving health services through the implementation of a Japanese-style quality management method known as 5S-KAIZEN-TQM. The 5S-Kaizen-TQM technique is a step-by-step quality promotion strategy that was initially applied in Japanese industry (mostly manufacturing businesses) as a continuous improvement strategy. This strategy is low-cost, yet it produces observable results in a fair amount of time, leading to customer and service provider satisfaction. This strategy has not completely applied in India. The studies conducted have been restricted to specific health care services, with no strategic framework for study on the implementation of organisational innovations in public health that demonstrate quality and efficiency yet defined.to fill this gap India call for projects related with 5s-kaizen-tqm implementation in healthcare. The purpose of this work is to evaluate how the introduction and distribution of the two stages 5S and KAIZEN may favourably influence the health sector, as well as the key factor influencing its success.

Tools used in 5s -kaizen- TQM approach

Several tools have been developed and others have been changed to facilitate efficient implementation of the 5S-KAIZEN-TQM Approach. The following are the tools:

- 5S-KAIZEN-TQM Monitoring and Evaluation sheet
- Action Plan Format
- KAIZEN Progress checklist
- Progress Report Format
- KAIZEN Process Checklist
- Five-S Activity Good Practice Sheet
- Example of Good Practice Sheet

Implementation Procedures of 5s-Kaizen-Tqm Approach in Health Sector

A pilot study must conduct to identify bout the situation in health care system and to implement the approach in the hospital. A field study was conducted to identify not only the inadequacies in departments in terms of the working environment and health care provision, but also the strengths that might be used to achieve goals. The diagnosis step resulted in the creation of a report that evaluated the existing condition. Given the nature of the method, which is primarily reliant on group work and the positive attitude of the team, this phase is critical to the approach's success and attainment of the predicted objectives. During the planning phase, a training session and introduction to the 5S - Kaizen method was held for the hospital A's heads of services and administrative employees. The 5S-Kaizen-TQM strategy was presented in a straightforward and effective manner, demonstrating the birth of the approach, clarifying the processes of implementation, and outlining the projected outcomes of this project. Then, a kick-off meeting with the staff of each pilot department was planned to disseminate the necessary information on the stages of the 5S approach's implementation and to share the vision and objectives to be achieved while emphasising the approach's keys to success: positive spirit and group work. Then, for each pilot service, a Quality Improvement Team (QIT) was restructured to provide frequent monitoring of the use of 5S, to ensure proper training for all workers, and to give the essential inputs for the 5S activities. All department profiles (head of department, quality manager, secretary, technician, hygiene and cleanliness manager, senior staff), administrative employees, and department heads were given to the QIT team. Finally, the training sessions were carryout for all departments.

Theoretical framework for 5S KAIZEN-TQM

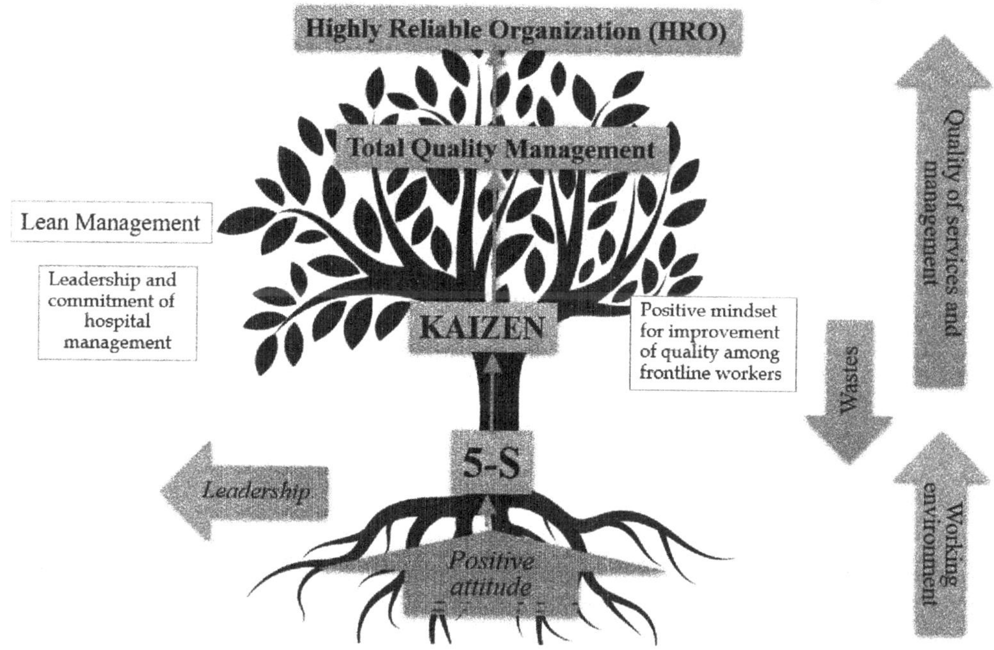

Discussions and Conclusions

African, American, and Asian countries used the 5S-Kaizen concept. We observe that the majority of these countries were interested in the first phase of this strategy: 5S. Kanamori et al. (Kanamori et al., 2016b) published a review of the literature on the implementation of 5S in hospitals in Brazil, India, Jordan, Senegal, Sri Lanka, Tanzania, the United Kingdom (UK), and the United States of America (USA), with a focus on (a) the context of its application, (b) its impacts, and (c) its adoption as part of government initiatives. These countries see 5S as a starting point for improving health-care quality. 67% of research investigated the influence of 5S and focused on three areas: safety, efficiency, and patient-centeredness. Literatures noted that 5S was adopted as part of government quality improvement strategies in Senegal, Sri Lanka, and Tanzania. Through JICA collaboration, 22 nations, including more than 500 health institutions, have embraced the concept across Africa, the Arab States, and Asia, boosting knowledge-sharing and co-creation among participants. Tanzania is a 5S-KAIZEN-TQM champion and a key nation in the organization's expansion throughout Africa. According to a recent JICA report, the country's hospital cleanliness, waste segregation, work environment, patient satisfaction, patient waiting time, incidence of phlebitis linked with intravenous cannulation, number of rejected laboratory samples, and patient overcrowding have all improved. Hospital income has grown as a result of improved utilisation of health insurance. JICA continues to support the model's knowledge-sharing and co-creation features by providing financial, technical, and logistical assistance (*Better Hospital Performance through 5S-KAIZEN-TQM - South-South Galaxy*, n.d.)

The hospital using the 5S-KAIZEN strategy in the teaching hospital saved time and effort, reduced work-related stress, reduced supply waste, increased staff and patient safety, and improved communication, efficiency, productivity, and problem-solving skill.(Hammami et al., 2022; Kanamori et al., 2016a). Hospitals employed colour codes and symbols to create a self-explanatory system for effective waste sorting. Bottom-up and top-down actions are combined in this method. Staff members play an important part in improving their work environment by removing waste and subsequently optimising processes via bottom-up actions. Workers are involved into top-down efforts to set the hospital's direction and to ensure horizontal links among various quality circles. Indeed, the involvement of employees who are familiar with what happens on the ground level in developing a top-down plan helps to the success of this method.(Hammami et al., 2022)

References

5S-Kaizen-TQM model for Quality Improvement of healthcare organization. (n.d.). Retrieved January 9, 2023, from https://www.linkedin.com/pulse/5s-kaizen-tqm-model-quality-improvement-healthcare-mitesh-soni

Better Hospital Performance through 5S-KAIZEN-TQM - South-South Galaxy. (n.d.). Retrieved January 12, 2023, from https://www.southsouth-galaxy.org/solution/better-hospital-performance-through-5s-kaizen-tqm/

Chiarini, A., Baccarani, C., & Mascherpa, V. (2018). Lean production, Toyota Production System and Kaizen philosophy: A conceptual analysis from the perspective of Zen Buddhism. *TQM Journal*, *30*(4), 425–438. https://doi.org/10.1108/TQM-12-2017-0178

Hammami, S., Hmida, F., Gharbi, H., Salah, A. ben, & Hamouda, C. (2022). Implementation the "5S-Kaizen-TQM" approach into public Hospital in Tunisia. *La Tunisie Médicale*, *100*(7), 503. /pmc/articles/PMC9703905/

Indian Healthcare Industry Analysis | IBEF. (n.d.). Retrieved January 9, 2023, from https://www.ibef.org/industry/healthcare-presentation

Islam, A., & Salam, A. (2022). Multiattribute Decision-Making of TQM Performance of Hospitals Using TQM Digraphs. *Mathematical Problems in Engineering*, *2022*. https://doi.org/10.1155/2022/3119888

Kanamori, S., Shibanuma, A., & Jimba, M. (2016a). Applicability of the 5S management method for quality improvement in healthcare facilities: A review. *Tropical Medicine and Health*, *44*(1), 1–8. https://doi.org/10.1186/S41182-016-0022-9/TABLES/1

Kanamori, S., Shibanuma, A., & Jimba, M. (2016b). Applicability of the 5S management method for quality improvement in health-care facilities: a review. *Tropical Medicine and Health*, *44*(1). https://doi.org/10.1186/S41182-016-0022-9

Maqbool, Adeel & Ahmad, Siraj. (2013). 5S-TQM Approaches to Medical Facilities in India: A Special Research Conducted on Medical Facilities in Lucknow Distt. Social Science Research Network. 1-14. 10.2139/ssrn.2349078.

Hasegawa, T. (2006). Study on organizational reinforcement through total quality management in the health and medical care sector. *Tokyo: JICA Institute for International Cooperation*.

Toyota Code of Conduct (March 2006), Toyota motor corporation (https://www.toyota-global.com/company/history_of_toyota/75years/common/pdf/code_of_conduct.pdf) (last accessed 2022-10-20

Safer, M., Bezouich, Z., Khelil, M., Zoghlami, C., & Arifa, N. (2018). Radiology department performance: case study of CT scan at Sahloul Hospital (Tunisia). *La Tunisie Medicale*, *96*(5), 281-286.

Hasegawa Toshihiko, Karandagoda Wimal, Édition Deuxième. Changement de management pour l'hôpital. *The Japan International Cooperation Agency (JICA) Edition.* 2013

ADULTS' ATTITUDES TOWARDS GOVERNMENTAL BANS ON SINGLE-USE PLASTIC BAGS AND AWARENESS ABOUT ENVIRONMENTAL HAZARDS MADE BY PLASTICS IN SOCIETY IN KERALA PERSPECTIVE WITH SPECIAL REFERENCE TO MALAPPURAM DISTRICT

Sini V T

Research Scholar, Research & PG Department of Commerce MES KEVEEYAM College, Valanchery Mobile No: 9539078855, E-Mail ID: sini000variyath@gmail.com

Dr Divya M

Assistant Professor, Research & PG Department of Commerce MES KEVEEYAM College, Mobile No: 8129772887, E-Mail ID: divyadcms@gmail.co

Single-use plastic products are inexpensive, widely accessible, and simple to use, making them very well-liked by individuals from all social classes. Plastic consumption, garbage production, and its inability to degrade all represent severe threats to the future of the environment worldwide. In the twenty-first century, governments all around the world started outlawing SUP altogether. As a part of this Government of Kerala decided to enforce a state wide ban on SUP from Januaray 1st 2020. But , the introduction of COVID-19 once more transformed the situation into a plastic pandemic. Demand and supply for SUP increased during the pandemic, and nations like India began to profit from this. After the peak of covid 19 pandemic Government of Kerala again imposed a restriction on SUP From July 1st 2022 This study aimed to understand the adults attitude towards Governments ban on single use plastic and awareness about environmental hazards made by these plastics among the respondents in Malappuram District of Kerala. Convenience sampling method is preferred for selecting samples and a structured questionnaire is used for collecting data.

Key words: Plastic Pollution, Single Use Plastic Product, Carry Bags, Awareness, Attitude, Environmental Hazard

Introduction

The word "plastic" is derived from the Greek word "Plastikos," which means "suited for moulding." It refers to materials that are pliable and synthetic or semi-synthetic in origin. Because they are long chain polymers, plastics contain inorganic substances like styrene, which adds to their non-biodegradable quality. The development of plastic was viewed as a practical replacement for wood, metal, and other biodegradable materials, a product that can reduce the consumption of quickly dwindling natural resources, and a way to protect the environment's biodiversity. However, that same plastic is now the biggest environmental hazard The product was produced indiscriminately in all forms due to its simplicity of manufacture and longevity, which were both seen as blessings. People have grown dependent on these plastic products to the point where it is challenging for them to stop using them unnecessarily, even after learning about the negative effects of plastic. Today, the biggest obstacle for everyone trying to safeguard the environment is the pollution brought on by discarded plastic products (Angriani & et al, 2020)

Reducing the usage of single-use plastic products is one of the finest methods to support environmental preservation. While the unscientific approach to waste management contributes to the environmental risk posed by single-use plastics, irresponsible individual behaviour is the other primary factor that leads to single-use plastics ending up as litter in the environment (Ghoshal, 2020 jan). Recent studies have shown that backyard burning of plasticgarbage is riskier than previously believed. Burning polystyrene polymers, such as cups, egg trays, plates, etc., emits styrene, a highly poisonous gas that is easily absorbed via the skinand lungs and has an impact on many different bodily systems. This raises the risk of cardiovascular diseases, exacerbates respiratory conditions, and negatively impacts the neurological, hepatic, renal, and other systems.

By creating social awareness and education, one can encourage a more eco-friendly approach and help shape a positive consumer behavior. However, the transformation can only happen gradually. There are no short-term training programs or awareness campaigns that can changethe longstanding habit of spontaneous choice of single-use plastic materials (Murthy, 2020). However, consistent positive reinforcement can help in the long run in curtailing waste generation and preventing littering. Eco-friendly behavior, which is necessary to reduce carbon dioxide emission, is the individual"s support of bans imposed by authorities or retailers to reduce the use of plastic bags and any innovative approaches that are adopted and consumers who are environmentally conscious and feel the social pressure, tend to reduce the use of plastic bags and switch to using cloth bags (Erkan Arı et al 2017). As a result of the above background, the purpose of the study was to determine the level of awareness, acceptance, and practice of plastic ban legislation among residents of the MalappuramDistrict of Kerala.

Significance of the study

Plastic bag is a serious problem all around the world. It creates Wastage problem, harms the environment and cause health hazards if being misused. However, people are still using it after its ban legislation by government. The research can be the charge of identifying why people prefer plastics after its ban legislation and their attitude towards this government bans. The significance of this study is to determine whether there is any correlation between adult consumers who typically rely heavily on single-use plastic products in their daily lives and their level of awareness of the risks associated with single-use plastics and their attitudes towards a plastic ban

Objectives of the study

1. To assess the level of consumer awareness regarding the plastic ban and the plasticpollution issue.
2. To identify the association between socio economic class of respondents and attitudetowards plastic ban
3. To examine consumers' attitudes towards alternatives to plastic bags, as well as thebarriers to their adoption.

Research design

A cross-sectional descriptive research based in a community was conducted. The study was conducted in the Malappuram district of Kerala, The sample consisted of all adult population in Malappuram District who have been habituated to use single use plastic products especially plastic bags for every day purchases. Using a systematic interviewer-administered questionnaire that had been pre-tested, information gathered from participants who were qualified and willing. Information about socio-demographic groups, such as age, gender, occupation, education, marital status and socio economic status were collected .The second part of questionnaire used to assess the awareness about the nature of hazards, pollution caused by single use plastic and the third part to assess the attitude towards governmental banon single use plastic. The responses were assessed using a 3 point scale . The content was analyzed by experts for validity and necessary changes done before the questionnaire was administered to the public. Collected data is analysed with the help of SPSS Softwareversuion 25.0

Results

The results of the study in the area of adults' attitudes towards governmental Bans on single- use plastic products and awareness about environmental hazards made by plasticsin society is conducted among 100 participants of adults in Malappuram district is presented in tablesand figures. Socio demographic profile of respondents is presented in table 1.

Table 1.1 Socio Demographic Profile of Respondents

S.no Number	Characteristic	%
1	Sex	
	Male	43.0
	Female	57.0
2	Age (in Years)	
	Below 30	33
	30-40	53

	40-50	14
3	Education	
	Up to SSLC	5
	Pre university	7
	Graduate	24
	Postgraduate	64
4	Occupation	
	Professional	63
	Skilled	6
	UnSkilled/Semi skilled	3
	Student	18
	Home Maker	10
5	Marital status	
	Married	77
	Unmarried	23
6	Socio economic class of family	
	Middle income	84
	Lower income	16

Participants of the study have belonged to the age group of below 30 and 40-50 range. Mean age of study participants is 1.81 which means that majority of the respondents have belongs to the age group of below 40. Female participants (57%) are more than male participants (43%). While analysing education (64%) respondents are post graduated, (24%) are graduated and (7%) are Pre university certificate holders and (5%) of them are SSLC. In socio economic aspect (84%) belongs to middle income and (16%) are from lower income. The occupational status of the study respondents nearly (63%) are professional, (6%) are skilled, (10%) are home makers and (18%) belongs to student category and (3%) are from semi-skilled/ unskilled.

Table 1.2 Awareness of hazards of plastic

Hazards of plastic	N	Mean	Std. Deviation
Use of plastic bags are hazardous to human health	100	2.77	0.617
Use of plastic bags leads to cancer	100	2.62	.693
It is possible to degrade plastic bags	100	2.31	.884

Air , Water and soil can be polluted by plastic	100	2.86	.513
It sustainable in long run	100	2.53	.731
Environmental dumping	100	2.55	.796

Table 1.2 shows , The awareness on hazards of plastic, Respondents are highly aware of the pollution caused by plastic, based on their mean score on the elements of awareness (2.86), followed by awareness regarding health hazardous due to plasti (Mean score 2.77). Additionally, most of them are aware that plastic exposure can cause cancer (2.62), Comparing awareness on possible degradation of plastic bags with other elements of awareness, we can conclude that awareness on possible degradation of plastic bags is lower(2.31)

Table 1.3 Attitude of respondents

Demographic Variables		Mean	S D	F value	P value
Education Qualification	Up to SSLC	2.9333	.09129	3.163	.028
	Pre university certificate	2.6667	.34694		
	Graduate	2.8611	.23399		
	Postgraduate	2.6953	.28414		
Occupation Status	Professional	2.7275	.29528	.453	.770
	Skilled	2.8333	.33333		
	UnSkilled/Semi skilled	2.8889	.19245		
	Student	2.7315	.19917		
	Home Maker	2.7833	.32442		
Age	Below 30	2.7374	.27013	.149	.862
	30-40	2.7579	.29700		
	40-50	2.7143	.25678		

Table 1.3 shows the result of ANOVA, in case of education the P value is less than .05, H0 is rejected at 5% level of significance. Hence concluded that there is a statistically significant difference among the education qualification with respect to awareness level of hazards of plastic.

A Tukey post-hoc test revealed that awareness level of hazards of plastic significantly lowerin case of graduate (2.66 ± .35 min, p=.04) and post graduate (2.69 ±.46 min, p=.034) level compare to the pre university level (2.66 ± .99). There were no statically significant difference between SSLC, graduate and post graduate group In case of occupation the null hypothesis is accepted at 5% level of significance, p value is morethan .05, (P-.770) there is no significant difference among occupation status and respondents attitude towards ban of plastic.ie respondents of different occupation category have same attitude towards ban of plastic.In case of age the null hypothesis is accepted at 5% level of significance, p value is more than.05, (P-.862) there is no significant difference among age and respondents attitude towards ban of plastic.ie respondents of different age group shows same attitude towards ban of plastic.

						value	
		High Level	Moderate Level	Low level		2.781	.249*
Income Level	Middle income	30	19	36	84		
	Lower income	5	6	5	16		
Gender	Male	12	14	17	43	3.426	.180*
	Female	23	10	24	57		
Marital status	Married	28	16	33	77	1.907	.385*
	Unmarried	7	8	8	23		

Table 1.4 Awareness Level of Respondent

In the lights of Pearson chi-square we accept the null hypothesis, P value is more than.05. It reveals thatthere is no statistically significant association between demographic variables (gender, marital status, socio economic class) and awareness level of respondents. That is, there is no difference in the awareness level of male and female, respondents of different socio economic class reveal approximately same level of awareness. Married and unmarried people shows equal level of awareness

Table 1.5 Reasons and Purpose for the Continued Use of Plastic Bags after its Ban

Reasons for continued use of plastic after its ban	**Percentage**
Easy to carry	67%
Easy to store	22%
Light weight	33%
Affordable	41%
Purpose of using plastic bags after its ban	**Percentage**
Local market	66%
Petty shop	24%
Fish market	71%
Textile shop	21%

Majority of the people continued the use of plastic bags after its ban, the reason behind thishabit is its convenience.(67%) respondents continued the use of plastic bags after its ban is it easiness to carry, followed by this (41%) of respondents preferred this due to its affordability and only (33%) of them prefer this due to its weightless nature.

People are continuing the use of plastic bags after its ban, they prefer these bags mainly from fish market (71%) and (66%) prefer this from local market, only (24%) prefer plastic bags from petty shops.

Table 1.6 Types of alternative bags preferred after ban of plastic bags

Types of alternative bags preferred after ban of plastic bags	Percentage
Cloth bags	77%
Paper bags	58%
Jute bags	18%

Majority(77%) of the respondents try to prefer cloth bags after the ban of plastic, and 58 % paper bags and only few 18% prefer jute bags.

Table 1.7 Problems faced by respondents due to ban of plastic

Problems faced by respondents due to ban of plastic	Percentage
Cost of bio-degradable alternatives	41%
Difficulties in using reusable bags	49%
Difficulties in identifying reusable ways	22%
Awareness on reusable alternatives	38%

Major (49%) problem faced by the respondents after the ban of plastic bag is difficulties in the substitution of reusable bags in all cases. 41% respondents say that cost of bio degradable alternative is the problem of plastic ban. Lack of awareness on reusable alternative is the other problem faced by respondents.

Discussion

Plastic is a serious hazard to both human health and the environment. This study which was conducted among 100 participants, the area of Malappuram district of Kerala, displays the present state of knowledge, acceptance, and practise about the use of plastic among the study participants following the passage of the plastic ban legislation, with a varied outcomes that is discussed below.

Awareness of plastic ban legislation among study participants

In the present study, 97% of study participants are aware of the plastic ban legislation. Out of them 94% accepted and agreed to use reusable bags and 80% of them advised others to stop the usage of plastic bags. Due to this awareness78% of them prefer shops which offer non plastic bags. While comparing with other studies made in

Delhi, Mangloore, etc study participants in Malappuram district of Kerala are more aware about plastic ban legislation. After this ban most of the respondents reduced the consumption of single use plastic products.

Awareness about health and environmental hazards due to plastic use

The majority of the subjects (100%) were aware of at least one health or environmental risk brought on by the use of plastic. These results are better when compared to different studies conducted in other parts of the world where only 50% to 70% of the respondents knew about the harmful health hazards on using plastic. 87% of Study participants were in the opinion of use of plastics are hazards to human health, but in same case 10% disagree with this. This may be due to the proper knowledge about harmful effect of plastic usage. To widen their knowledge, there are posters and banners published the negative repercussions of plastic use printed on them.

Reason for the continued use of plastic Bags

According to this study, people preferred plastic bags after its ban due to their easiness to carry (67%) , affordability (41%), light weight (33%), and easy to store (22%). This has been just about similar to the study results made in Manglore and Delhi. Easy availability is the reason for its continued usage in Manglore and convenience for shopping are the reason found in study conducted in Delhi. Even so affordability and easy availability are the reasons in Ethiopian studies. When compare to the present study it states that only 44% prefer this due to affordability.

Practices for alternative bag usage

It was noticed that 77% of the subjects shifted to the use of cloth bags and 18 % preferred jute bags, but the point is that 58% prefer paper bags in certain cases but its not an effective substitute for plastic bags. None of them prefer baskets instead of plastic bags. Its observed that absolute substitution of eco-friendly alternatives for plastic bags is not achieved yet. The study found that despite all these developments, there is still a gap at the implementation level.In light of this, awareness campaigns are ineffective in disseminating information about the penalties imposed under this legislation, as well as the lack of community involvement.Sothe only solution before the very eyes of government is to take initiatives for developing biodegradable platics which are free from evils of single use plastic.

Purpose of using plastic bags after its ban

Best part of the study participants continued the use of plastic bags after its ban even if they were aware about the same. Most of them prefer this in case of purchases in fish market (71%), a slight difference was shown in the matter of local market (66%). Hardly ever prefer these in case of textile shops (21%), because they offer biodegradable substitutes, in the matter of pretty shop only 24% is preferred.

Problems faced by the respondents due to ban of plastic

It was observed that respondents faces some difficulties due to the ban of plastic. In the lights of present study difficulties in using reusable bags (49%), cost of bio-degradable alternatives (41%) lack of awareness on reusable bags (38%) and difficulties in identifying reusable ways (22%) are the main obstacles faced by them. For the sake of society influence of these obstacles could be weakened by conducting awareness campaigns. Local self-governments should take initiatives for the same.

Associated factors of the plastic use

In the present study participants among the age group of 30-40 shows a positive attitude towards the ban of plastic when compared to the age group of below 30 and above 40. The findings of this study contradict those of a study conducted in Delhi, which found that youngsters were more aware of plastic bags' harmful effects. While making a gender wise analysis of awareness of hazards of plastic it shows that male participants are more aware of the evils of plastic. This out-turn also reflected in the part of *continued use of plastic bags after its ban,* Females are use its more than male. By comparing these results with previous studies significant differences are visible. There are differences in the implementation of the ban in different districts, which illustrates the complexity of the issue

Conclusion

The study shows better awareness (97%) about the plastic ban legislation. Satisfactory awareness level about the ill effects of plastic use and its ban was observed but the level of implementation in their daily life was poor. Most part of the respondents continued the use of plastic bags after its bans. The findings underscore the need for an improved attitude and practice regarding the use of eco-friendly alternatives in lieu of plastic. Most of the participants in the settings had the awareness of health hazards of the usage of plastic bags and supported its ban. However, practices with respect to usage of alternative bags or reuse ofalready used bags were found poor among majority of the participants.

Recommendations

Organize intensified awareness programme to the Public, especially students and homemakers. Discount on products can be offered for customers who bring their own environmentally friendly bags. Initiatives should take to develop biodegradable plastic bags and other plastic products. It is possible to initiate measures for the scientific disposal of plastic products.

REFERENCE

Angriani, p., & et al. (2020). Ban on Plastic Bags Usage: Consumer Perception of Single-Use Plastic Bags in Traditional Market. *roceedings of the 2nd International Conference on Social SciencesEducation. 525*, pp. 226-232. Advances in Social Science, Education and Humanities Research.

Ghoshal, P. M. (2020 jan). A Research Report on Single Used Plastic Carry Bags and Its. Delhi.Jalil, M. A., &

et al. (2013). using plastic bags and its damaging impact on Environment and Agricultuire: An Alternative Proposal. *International Journal of Learning & Development, 3*(4).

Kumar, J. N., & et al. (2016). A study to asees awareness level and perception about legislationamong a small population of Manglore city. *10*(4).

Murthy, M. (2020). Economy vs Environmrnt Single Use Plastic (SUP) Ban in India. *Hpnlu journal of environment and disaster management,* 28-41.

P, S., & et al. (2020 Jan). Awareness, acceptance and practice of plastic ban legislation among residents of an urban area in Kanchipuram district, Tamil Nadu:a cross sectional study.*International Journal of Community Medicine and Public Health, 7*(1), 256-263.

Philips, W., & et al. (n.d.). Economic implications of the ban on single-use plastics in the Caribbean.(n.d.).

The Impact of awareness about environmental hazards caused by plastic pollution, on the attitude towards governmental ban on single use plastic products among adults in the Indian City Chennai and its suburbs. (2019). *Online Journal of Multidisciplinary Subjects, 13*(1), 156-167.

Single-Use Plastic Bans: Exploring Stakeholder Perspectives on Best Practices for Reducing PlasticPollution. 81(8),(2021).

GREEN ACCOUNTING: EXPLORING THE CONCEPT AND LEGAL FRAMEWORK IN INDIAN SCENARIO

Unais P

Research Scholar, Department of Commerce & Management Studies

PSMO College, Tirurangadi

Dr. Abdul Naser V

Assistant Professor, Department of Commerce & Management Studies

PSMO College, Tirurangadi

Abstract

Corporate social responsibility today places a great deal of emphasis on environmental protection. Promoting economic growth and preserving the environment are the twin problem that the world is now dealing with. Most industrial and corporate houses throughout the world are implementing the notion of environmental factor into their company operations in order to thrive in this fiercely competitive market. Using green accounting, an organisation will be able to measure how much a specific industry is consuming and how much it is costing the environment. Essentially, green accounting is a system new accounting practise that records the costs and benefits of the eco system to a business. In accounting, green accounting also known as environmental accounting has become a new challenge. This paper aims to uncover the concept of green accounting in India as well as its legal framework. The study also examines the practices of corporate level environmental accounting as well as its associated problems.

Key words: *Green accounting, Environmental reporting, Corporate Social responsibility, Environmental accounting,*

Introduction

Protecting the environment and fostering economic growth are two issues that emerging nations like India must simultaneously address. A necessary trade-off should be made between environmental preservation and development. Finding the safe boundaries of environmental deterioration and the appropriate degree of growth requires a detailed evaluation of the advantages and costs of environmental damages. Green/Environmental accounting is a useful tool for understanding how business enterprises interact with the environment and contribute to environmental safety and welfare. It offers information that highlights both the benefits that commercial firms provide to the economy and the costs that are incurred due to the depletion of resources and pollution.

Since the previous 50 years, economic policy-making has relied heavily on measures like Gross Domestic Product (GDP) and Net Domestic Product (NDP). These measures are a part of the national income accounting that each nation has created. The reality that the economy cannot function in a black box was overlooked by these conventional measures of economic activity. As a result, the national accounts allow for the depreciation of man-made assets, but do not allow for the depreciation of environmental assets because their economic contribution is not assessed. The practise of Green accounting, sometimes referred to as "environmental accounting," aims to include environmental expenses into business operations' financial outcomes. Since the environment is ignored by Gross Domestic Product, decision-makers requires a new model that takes green accounting into consideration. In this paper, the national accounts are briefly reviewed, their flaws and how to construct better indicators of human well-being are discussed, followed by limitations to green accounting and government policies regarding them.

Statement of the Problem

Green accounting is a crucial tool for comprehending how the environment interacts with the economy. In India, environmental accounting is still in its infancy. The present study is being performed to build a theoretical model of green accounting, reporting procedures used by Indian corporations, and legal framework for Indian corporations.

Objectives of the Study

The following issues might be used to illustrate the study's objectives:

1. To analyse the traditional accounting system and pinpoint its shortcomings.
2. To draw attention to the necessity of green accounting in India.
3. To identify the main challenges to the sound growth of green accounting.
4. To draw attention to the relevant government initiatives in this field.

Methodology

This study is descriptive in nature and based on secondary data. The internet, books, journals, and published papers are the sources of secondary data.

Evolution of Green National Accounting

1. System of National Accounts

Green national accounting may be seen as an expansion of the basic idea of national economic accounts, which was codified in the Standard National Accounts (SNA) framework. This was derived from research conducted by James Meade and Richard Stone during World War II and is described in the paper as follows:

NNP = C + I – D + X – M

Where,

NNP = Net National Product

C = Consumption

I = Investment

D = Depreciation

X = Exports

M = Imports

Thus, an open economy's Net National Product consists Consumption in addition to Net Investments (Investment – Depreciation) and Net Exports (Exports – Imports).

Since all changes in non-produced natural assets between opening and closing stocks are explained in the SNA as holding profits or losses and other changes in asset volume, the parts of the column linked to non-produced economic assets are not taken into account when calculating NDP. Therefore, the items classified under "other changes in volume" are the most significant ones to be reclassified for assessment in the accounting for natural resources.

2. Shortcomings of the Traditional System of Accounting

The following is a summary of the primary issues with traditional national accounts that were discussed earlier:

i. The conventional approaches mostly neglected the non-marketed services offered by natural resources in favour of the products and services that are traded on markets. For instance, forests offer a wide range of environmental services, such as flood control, protection against soil erosion, carbon sequestration, and amenity benefits, in addition to producing commercial goods like wood for fuel and lumber. National accounting solely take into consideration the economic value of trees and neglect the benefits to the ecosystem. The environmental sector's waste disposal services are also not included in the national accounts.

ii. Both natural and man-made resources are handled inconsistently. As previously indicated, man-made machinery is depreciated to provide for replacement of losses in the capital stock when sustainable income measurements like net national product or net domestic product are computed. Losses in the natural resources, however, are not discounted in the same way. The national accounts, for instance, do not account for the loss to society as a result of the transfer of forests when they are used for non-forest activities; they simply record the cost of clear-cutting the forests. In furthermore, decline in forest area. is reflected in other volume changes that have no impact on GDP.

iii. These measurements, such as GDP and NDP, are insufficient to capture the state of the environmental degradation. Environmental quality restoration costs are sometimes included as gains in national revenue and output. For instance, increases to GDP are shown for activities such as cleaning up rivers, purifying water for consumption, and spending in advance to safeguard against the negative consequences of pollution.

Therefore, the existing national income measures are insufficient as indices of social wellbeing and also give incorrect information about whether a country's economy is utilising its resources responsibly. Environmental accounting can therefore be helpful in eliminating the biases that are present today.

Green Accounting

The term "green accounting," sometimes known as "environmental accounting," "resource accounting," or "integrated economic and environmental accounting," describes accounting procedures that take into consideration the costs, affects, and repercussions of the environment. It is about data aggregation that connects the company's financials to the environment, which will undoubtedly have a long-term influence on both the organization's economic and environmental strategy. It involves more than just performing social cost-benefit analyses of various firm initiatives or activities or valuing the output of environmental goods and services. An effort is being made to identify and depict the depleted resources and costs that organisations have contributed to the environment. Transparency about environmental costs in accounts is the main goal of green accounting.

Types of Environmental Accounting

1. **Environmental Management Accounting (EMA):** This approach placed a strong emphasis on management accounting, paying particular attention to data on the flow of materials and energy as well as environmental costs. The following subsystems can be used to further categorise this form of accounting:

a. **Segment Environmental Accounting:** This is an internal environmental accounting tool used to pick a project or investment activity pertaining to environmental preservation from among all operational processes and evaluate the effects on the environment over a predetermined time frame.

b. **Corporate Environmental Accounting:** PDCA for sustainable environmental management activities is supported by this internal environmental accounting instrument.

c. **Eco-Balance Environmental Accounting:** This is a tool to educate the general public about important data gathered in compliance with the Environmental Accounting. For this reason, it utilizes the cost and effect (in terms of quantity and money value) of its environmental conservation operations.

2. **Environmental Financial Accounting (EFA):** This approach with financial accounting as its basic form, focuses on reporting environmental liability and costs, along with other significant environmental costs.

3. **Environmental National Accounting (ENA):** Based on National Level Accounting, this method is focused on natural resource stocks and flows, externality cost and environmental costs etc.

Scope of Green Accounting

Green accounting consists of estimating environmental costs and expenses, capitalising those costs, identifying environmental liabilities, and measuring environmental liabilities.

- **Environmental costs and expenses**

These are expenditures or costs associated with environmental measures, such as production-related costs and product development costs, which are incurred primarily to ensure environmental protection.

- **Capitalization of environmental costs**

Capitalization of environmental expenditures is justified if the expense lengthens the life, boosts the capacity, enhances the effectiveness, or increases the safety of property owned by the company, mitigates or prevents environmental contamination, improves the resource similar to its condition at the time of acquisition, or is incurred in connection with getting the property ready for sale.

- **Environmental liabilities**

Obligation to make future payments in order to repair environmental harm caused by earlier events, activities, or transactions, or to make up for losses experienced by a third party. It could even involve a contingent environmental obligation that is dependent on the existence or absence of one or more unpredictable future occurrences or a duty to make amends to a third party who has endured such harm.

- **Measurement of Environment liabilities**

Both quantitative and non-quantifiable environmental liabilities are possible. If it is a measurable liability, meaning one whose worth can be precisely measured, include it in the balance sheet; otherwise, provide a footnote outlining the details of the responsibility.

Environmental Accounting: A Need for the Business World

It is useful to understand whether a firm has been upholding its environmental obligations. A firm must primarily satisfy the following environmental obligations:

- Conforming to the regulatory standards or surpassing those expectations.
- Letting present and future investors know the kind, scope, and extent of the management's protective actions.
- Cleaning up existing pollution and effectively getting rid of the dangerous substances.
- Working to prevent the occurrence of those environmental costs and compensation.
- Control over rising expenses for waste management, raw materials, and possible liabilities.

- Control over material and operational efficiency advantages resulting from a highly competitive global market.
- Promoting a business with a strong environmental stance.

Limitations and Challenges

Although many nations are attempting environmental accounting, there are significant limitations and challenges with the idea. The following are the main challenges and limitations facing environmental accounting and reporting:

1. The methodology used to determine the social value of environmental goods and services is ineffective, frequently deceptive, and inaccurate.
2. Estimated values for environmental products that have been defined or measured in terms that cannot be directly converted to money.
3. Environmental accountings are not valuable economically.
4. Because environmental expenses are not recorded and it is difficult to extract and separate environmental costs, the data from the industry is extremely unreliable.
5. Environmental accounting lacks accounting standards.
6. The estimations are likely to be out of date before they can be put to use since the social value placed on environmental products and services is changing so quickly.
7. Impractical assumptions.
8. Absence of trustworthy industry data.
9. In the majority of circumstances, environmental accounting is not required by law in India.
10. There is no set procedure for accounting. If the accounting technique used by two companies or nations differs, comparisons between the two cannot be made, which is rather obvious.

Green Accounting Practices in India

1. Very few businesses provide sufficient information about environmental issues. They compile and submit any necessary environmental information if required to do so by the applicable law. In this respect, the Environment Ministry has given instructions on how to draft. They mostly provide the following sorts of information an environmental statement.

i. The kind of pollution control equipment deployed.
ii. Measures done to conserve energy.
iii. Measures taken for conservation of raw materials.
iv. Measures taken for production process waste and waste water.

v. Measures done to improve the quality of goods and services, the manufacturing process, etc.

2. According to Mohiuddin et. al. (2018), the business community is completely aware of the criteria for environmental reporting. They are also conscious of the problem with the environment. The corporate CEOs have also voiced their support for industries reporting on the environment. Despite their understanding and permission, industries' environmental reporting is very lacking. The annual report has remarkably little information since it is so lacking.

3. Research studies have looked at the volume of social information that businesses create, which includes environmental information. The following are some general themes that result from this:

i. There are few firms that disclose, and the amount of information is small.

ii. The degree of disclosure varies over time, between nations, and between businesses. The changing business climate and the social, economic, and political environments in which they take place are reflected in social disclosure in general and environmental disclosure in particular. However, the overall volume of voluntary disclosure remains mostly stable over time, but the subject covered in the disclosure varies.

iii. There is a very clear size impact, with bigger organisations being more likely to disclose than smaller ones.

iv. Very little of the disclosure will actually contain figures, whether financial or otherwise, and very little of it will qualify as information by any conventional standards.

4. Furthermore, it was discovered that the majority of businesses provide environmental information in a descriptive manner rather than according to financial means, i.e., corporate profits are calculated without taking into consideration the deterioration of natural capital.

Legal Framework for Environmental Accounting in India

Industrial licencing has, for all purposes, been abolished, but environmental approval from multiple government agencies now occupies the forefront. India has established a Union Ministry of Environment with the goal of coordinating environmental protection and antipollution actions across the states and the other ministries in response to growing worldwide concern about environmental protection. It has also enacted the necessary laws. Here are some of the laws that are pertinent to environmental protection:

i. Directly related to environment protection:

a) The Environment (Protection) Act, 1986

b) The Forest (Conservation) Act, 1980

c) The Air (Prevention and Control of Pollution) Act, 1981

d) Water (Prevention and Control of Pollution) Cess Act, 1977

e) Water (Prevention and Control of Pollution) Act, 1974

ii. Indirectly related to environment protection:

a) The National Environment Tribunal Act, 1995

b) Public Liability Insurance Act, 1991

c) Motor Vehicle Act, 1991

d) Hazardous Waste (Management & Handling) Rules, 1989

e) Indian Fisheries Act, 1987

f) Merchant of shipping Act, 1958

g) Merchant of shipping Act, 1958

h) Constitutional provision (Article 51A)

i) Indian Port Act

j) Indian Penal Code

Conclusion

One of the key facets of today's corporate social responsibility is social responsibility regarding the environment. Most industrial and corporate houses throughout the world are embracing the concept of environmental element in their company operations in order to survive in this competitive market. These industrial establishments have a distinct understanding of the need to include environmental considerations into their operations in addition to high standards of quality if they are to succeed in their respective industries. In India, environmental accounting is still in its early stages. Very few businesses provide sufficient information about environmental issues. India's population is inadequately educated about environmental safety, and the growth of accounting in this area is rather dubious. The industries should concentrate on and put aside a portion of their resources for ecological balance and environmental conservation. Therefore, it is required of corporate entities to account for the usage of substances that might harm the environment. Environmental accounting and reporting face a number of difficulties, including social values in relevant assumptions, economic value, and a lack of trustworthy industrial data. It is high time for corporations to have a strong environmental policy, implement pollution control measures, adhere to relevant laws and regulations, and adequately describe environmental issues in annual reports.

REFERENCES

1. Rahim, A & Heba, Y. (2010), Green accounting –a proposition for EA/ER conceptual implementation methodology, Journal of Sustainability and Green Business, Green Accounting, 1-18.
2. Ahmad, N. N. N. and Sulaiman, M. (2004). Environmental disclosures in Malaysian annual reports: A legitimacy theory perspective. International Journal of Commerce and Management, 14(1), 41–57.
3. Pramanik, A. K., Shil, N. C. and Das, B., (2007), Environmental Accounting and Reporting with Special Reference to India.

4. Banarjee, B (2006). Corporate Environmental Accounting and Reporting, The Chartered Accountant, April 2006. 720 – 727.
5. Akbas H. E. and Canikli, S. (2014): Corporate Environmental Disclosures in a Developing Country: An Investigation on Turkish Listed Companies: International Journal of Economics and Finance; Vol. 6, No. 2.
6. Paul, K. C. and Pal, B. (2001): Corporate Environmental Reporting in India. Indian Accounting Review, (December), 27-45
7. Quareshi, N. Z., Kulshrestha, D, and Bhushantiwari., S., "Environmental Accounting and Reporting: An Essential Component of Business Strategy", Asian Journal of Research in Banking and Finance, Vol 2, Issue 4, April 2012.
8. Rahman, M. A. and Muttakin, M. B. (2005). Corporate Environmental Reporting Practices in Bangladesh – A Study of Some Selected Companies. The Cost & Management, 33(4), 13-21.
9. Singh, G., Joshi, M., (2009) Environment management and disclosure practices of Indian companies, International Journal of Business Research.
10. Gray., R and Bebbington., J. (2001) Accounting for the Environment, SAGE Publications.
11. Mohiuddin, M., Al Mamun, A., Syed, F., Mehedi Masud, M., & Su, Z. (2018). Environmental Knowledge, Awareness, and Business School Students' Intentions to Purchase Green Vehicles in Emerging Countries. Sustainability, 10(5), 1534.

ATTITUDE AND INTENTION OF THE POST GRADUATE STUDENTS TOWARDS THE ENTREPRENEURSHIP

Muhammed Asif V, Muhammed Asjad C K, Muhammed Safwan
Bachelor of Commerce, Sullamussalam Science College, Areekode

Suhail P, Ahammed Fayas T
Assistant Professor, Sullamussalam Science College, Areekode
PG Department of Commerce, Sullamussalam Science College, Areekode

ABSTRACT

Entrepreneurial intention refers to individual's states of mind that aimed at creating new venture, developing new business concept or creating new value within existing firms. It is an important factor in facilitating towards new venture establishment and has significant impact on the firms 'venture success, survival and growth'. Studies have shown that the favourable attitude towards business or entrepreneurship result in strengthening the intention to become a powerful and successful entrepreneur in the future. India is not a country of employment jobs but a country of endless enterprise opportunities. There are not one million jobs but ten million work opportunities. A nation's ability to generate a steady stream of business opportunities can only come about when its people take to entrepreneurial activities. Thus, this study sought to explore factors affecting the entrepreneurial intention among post graduate students of the aided colleges, which are conveniently selected by the researchers from a selected region. The study has addressed many dimensions of the entrepreneurial behaviour and attitudes like personal attributes, subjective norms, and entrepreneurial self-efficiency of the respondents through this present research work. For that purpose, the study has collected 100 and more samples data from the PG students. The data collection has been carried out through a structured questionnaire which are distributed directly to the participants as well as through the online platforms also. Based on the appropriate statistical tools and techniques, the study has found that there are many key factors which are influencing the entrepreneurship intentions among the students to become a popular entrepreneur in the future. The present study will give an outline about how the entrepreneurship characters are building among the students and which different factors are influencing the students towards the concept of entrepreneurship. The output also reveals an important message to the educational institutions to focus and incorporate some quality measurements to ensure the students tastes on the entrepreneurship which are maintained and progressed through their education practices.

Keywords: Entrepreneurship, Attitudes, Intentions, Students

Introduction

No matter if a country is considered to have a mature economy, an emerging economy, or a developing economy, entrepreneurial endeavours are essential to the growth of their respective economies. Students from today's generation are going to be the country's business leaders of the future. People believe that entrepreneurial activity will benefit the economy and may make a significant contribution to the country's overall wealth in the future. Many people who graduate from college are unable to find job that is appropriate for the level of education they earned. The study of entrepreneurship as a distinct branch of science is a relatively new development. It is still trying to discover its niche and identify analytical paradigms that are distinctly different from the domains of theory of the firm in economics and behavioural aspects in management studies. This is something that it has been working on for quite some time.

In order to conduct a study on the attitudes and intentions of postgraduate (PG) students towards entrepreneurship, it is likely that a sample of PG students would be surveyed in order to collect data on their perceptions of entrepreneurship, their level of interest in beginning a business, and their plans to pursue entrepreneurship in the future. The survey would most likely include questions about factors that may influence respondents' attitudes and intentions, such as respondents' levels of education and previous experience with entrepreneurship, as well as respondents' perceptions of the entrepreneurship ecosystem in their local community. The findings of the research might be put to use to determine which aspects of entrepreneurship teaching and support for postgraduate students need to be enhanced, as well as to get a better understanding of how to more effectively engage and support prospective student entrepreneurs.

The studies that are found in the literature review are likely to investigate various aspects of postgraduate students' behaviours and intentions towards entrepreneurship. These aspects may include the students' perceptions of entrepreneurship, their level of interest in beginning a business, and their plans to pursue entrepreneurship in the future. Some studies may also investigate factors that may influence participants' attitudes and intentions, such as the participants' levels of education, the extent to which they have previous experience with entrepreneurship, and their perceptions of the entrepreneurship ecosystem in their local community.

In this context, "Entrepreneurial intention" refers to the mental states of individuals that are focused towards the creation of new ventures, the development of new business concepts, or the creation of new value within enterprises that already exist. It plays a vital role in aiding the development of new ventures and has a considerable influence on the firms "venture success, survival, and growth.' Studies have demonstrated that having a positive attitude about business and entrepreneurship results in a strengthened ambition to become a powerful and successful entrepreneur in the future. India is not a country with a large number of employment prospects but rather a country with limitless business opportunities. It is more accurate to say that there are ten million employment opportunities rather than one million jobs. Only when the people of a country engage in entrepreneurial activity will that country be able to produce a consistent flow of possibilities for company owners to pursue (Arnold, 2022).

Objectives of the study

1) To study the Personal Attitudes of the students towards the Entrepreneurship.
2) To examine the Intentions of the students towards the Entrepreneurship.
3) To Study the elements of subjective norms related to the student's entrepreneurship Intention
4) To evaluate the Entrepreneurial self-efficiency among the students.
5) To examine the role of personal attitude, subjective norms and self-efficiency of the PG students towards their Entrepreneurship intention

Review of literature

S. Arunkumar, J. Jose Prabhu, S. Divya, V. Sangari, S. Nandhini, R. Prasanna, and S.Prakash (2018) made an effort to investigate the ways in which the entrepreneurial mindset of an individual varies from that of other people. The findings of the study showed that students, on average, have a good attitude towards entrepreneurial endeavours, and that these findings impact positive attitudes. The researchers proposed that the educational establishment should encourage students to explore becoming entrepreneurs, with the expectation that these individuals will start their own businesses in order to have greater freedom in their personal and family lives. According to the findings of the study conducted by Fasla N P (2017), the vast majority of students believe that engaging in entrepreneurial activity is a positive thing to do. The current system of management education does not place an emphasis on the development of entrepreneurialism. Their research demonstrates that entrepreneurial mindsets are prevalent among students, as shown by Magdalena Raczynska and Adam Krystian Wisniewski's (2016) study. The research reveals that the vast majority of respondents considered themselves to be entrepreneurial, which is likely the reason why so many respondents have entertained the idea of starting their own company. They did so because they had the misconception that running your own company may bring in greater profits than doing a normal job full time.

Evan D. (2005) explored the effect of entrepreneurial attitudes and entrepreneurial self-efficacy on an individual's desire to participate in entrepreneurial behaviour. Specifically, he was interested in how these factors influence an individual's likelihood of starting their own business. According to the findings, those who value higher levels of income and independence as well as greater levels of ownership tend to have high levels of entrepreneurial aspirations. According to the findings of the study, there is no connection between risk prosperity and entrepreneurial ambitions. The researchers Souitaris, Zerbinati, and Andreas (2007) found that entrepreneurship education stimulates students' subjective norms and intention towards entrepreneurship. This is accomplished by providing students with the knowledge, skills, and sense of beliefs that inspire students to choose entrepreneurship as a career path. In a study conducted by Grid et al. (2008), the theory of planned behaviour was investigated for its potential as a predictor of entrepreneurial intention among students in their last year of study in commerce at two institutions in the Western Cape. The study looked at a variety of factors that may be used to predict an individual's intention to start a business. There was not a substantial contribution made by personal characteristics, demographic factors, or situational factors to the variation that was described by the theory of planned behaviour.

Intentional models have received criticism for their linear and static approach since the dawn of the twenty-first century. One the one hand, they failed to consider mediating effects between the suggested scales that might have indirect impacts on the endogenous variable (Izaias & Pablo, 2020; Syed, Butler, Smith, & Cao, 2020). Similar to this, the entrepreneurial intention variable is dynamic, meaning that new factors may affect the firms and have an impact on it. We have concentrated on the attitude towards entrepreneurial behaviour as a determining component in the students' entrepreneurial ambitions in an effort to fill up some of these gaps. It has been demonstrated that people's attitudes towards this goal improve and have a favourable impact on their entrepreneurial intention when they believe they have the capacity and authority to operate a business (Zhao, Lei, He, Gu, & Li, 2015). Other writers have demonstrated how a more positive attitude towards the entrepreneurial aim might indirectly impact one's view of one's capacity to operate a business (Prabhu, McGuire, Drost, & Kwong, 2012). According to Wang et al., self-control and attitude judgements should be used as a mediator of entrepreneurial intention (Wang, Chang, Yao, & Liang, 2016). Additionally, there is student research on the tangential associations between students' intentions to become entrepreneurs and their perceptions of capacity and control (Zhao et al., 2015).

Research Methodology

The present study has followed descriptive research design to explain the characteristics of a population based on the selected sample. The study has used primary data and collected 90 responses from post graduate students from Areekode Panjayath, based on the convenient sampling technique. A structured questionnaire was distributed to the respondents and collected their remarks through an online survey technique. Percentage analysis and multiple regression analysis are the major statistical tools used for the data analysis.

Results and Discussions

Under this section, the study deals with five major research objectives and the results and discussions of the same are given below.

Table 1: Personal attitude of students towards entrepreneurship

Statement	Frequency	Percentage
Strongly not infleuncing	4	4.44
Not infleuncing	17	18.89
Neutral	24	26.67
Infleuncing	35	38.89
Strongly influencing	10	11.11
Total	**90**	**100.00**

According to the statistics presented in the table above, the personal attitudes of approximately 39 percent of the students, or 35 out of 90, have a positive influence on the entrepreneurial behaviour of other students.

Table 2: Entrepreneurship intentions among the PG student

Statement	Frequency	Percentage
Highly not intrested	4	4.44
Not intrested	16	17.78
Neutral	36	40.00
Intrested	22	24.44
Highly intrested	12	13.33
Total	**90**	**100.00**

The observations presented in the table above reveals that forty percent of the students, or 36 out of 90, do not have a strong preference either way regarding the prospect of starting their own business in the future.

Table 3: Subjective norms related to the entrepreneurship behavior

Statement	Frequency	Percentage
Never support	6	6.67
No support	21	23.33
Neutral	40	44.44
Low support	19	21.11
High support	4	4.44
Total	**90**	**100.00**

The findings of this study provide an indication of whether or not the significant others in the PG students' lives will support their decision to become entrepreneurs in the future. In this case, 44.44% of people responded that they do not have an opinion, which indicates that they are uncertain about that.

Table 4: Entrepreneurial self-efficiency of the student

Statement	Frequency	Percentage
Highly not efficient	4	4.44
Not efficient	28	31.11
Neutral	32	35.56
Efficient	20	22.22
Highly efficient	6	6.67
Total	**90**	**100.00**

According to these findings, 35.56 percent of students believe that they do not have a strong opinion either way about their potential to become successful business owners.

Table 5. Regression Analysis Output

	Entrepreneurial Intentions	Correlation Sig. (2-tailed)	R	R Square	Adjusted R Square	F ratio (ANOVA)	Sig.	Standardized Coefficients (Beta)	Sig. value
Entrepreneurial Intentions	1.000								
Personal Attitude	.673	.000	.708 a	.501	**.483**	28.744	**.000b**	**0.511**	**0.000**
Subjective Norms	.348	.000						**-0.032**	**0.724**
Self-efficacy	.594	.000						**0.282**	**0.005**

Dependent variable: Entrepreneurial Intentions

Independent variables: Personal Attitude, Subjective Norms, and Self-efficacy

According to the table's research results, the three independent variables can contribute for 48.3% of the variance in the entrepreneurship intention of PG students.

Findings, Implications, and Conclusion

Personal attitudes held by the student have been shown to have a positive influence on entrepreneurial activity. The vast majority of the students have an interest in going into business for themselves in the future. Students who are unsure whether or not they will receive support from their family and friends in their aspirations to start their own business. Students are also experiencing a sense of uncertainty regarding their level of self-efficiency with regard to entrepreneurship. In general, the three factors of personal attitudes, subjective norms, and self-efficiency are playing a greater role in the entrepreneurial intentions of postgraduate students.

Since the students have such a strong interest in starting their own businesses, the academic curriculum ought to be revised so that it includes more topics that motivate students to start their own businesses. The focus of educational institutions should be on providing students with a variety of opportunities to improve their skills so that students can feel more confident in their ability to pursue entrepreneurial endeavours. The mindset of society as a whole needs to be shifted in a constructive direction towards entrepreneurship, and everyone in the community needs to lend immediate support to each and every one of the students' business ideas.

References

Arnold, D. C. (2022). All 'Shook'up: Bob Hope, the USO, and How a Night in Greenland Changed Television. *Historical Journal of Film, Radio and Television*, *42*(2), 286-310.

Arunkumar, S., Prabhu, J. J., Divya, S., Sangavi, V., Nandhini, S., Prasanna, R., & Prakash, S. (2018). Entrepreneurial attitude among management students: an empirical study. *International Journal of Pure and Applied Mathematics*, *119*(7), 2389-2398.

Evan, D. (2005). Individual Intentions towards entrepreneurship Vs Entrepreneurship. *University of Sunshine Coast, Sippy Downs, Australia5.*

Fasla, N. P. (2017). A Study on entrepreneurship attitude among college students. *International Journal of Research Science & Management*, *4*(4), 53-59.

Gosens, J., Hellsmark, H., Kåberger, T., Liu, L., Sandén, B. A., Wang, S., & Zhao, L. (2018). The limits of academic entrepreneurship: Conflicting expectations about commercialization and innovation in China's nascent sector for advanced bio-energy technologies. *Energy Research & Social Science*, *37*, 1-11.

Martins, I., & Perez, J. P. (2020). Testing mediating effects of individual entrepreneurial orientation on the relation between close environmental factors and entrepreneurial intention. *International Journal of Entrepreneurial Behavior & Research*, *26*(4), 771-791.

Qiu, S., Yang, W. Z., Yao, C. L., Qiu, Z. D., Shi, X. J., Zhang, J. X., ... & Guo, D. A. (2016). Nontargeted metabolomic analysis and "commercial-homophyletic" comparison-induced biomarkers verification for the systematic chemical differentiation of five different parts of Panax ginseng. *Journal of Chromatography A*, *1453*, 78-87.

Raczyńska, M., & Wiśniewski, A. K. (2016). Entrepreneurial Attitudes among Students. Research Results. *Acta Universitatis Nicolai Copernici. Zarządzanie*, *43*(3), 101-111.

Souitaris, V., Zerbinati, S., & Al-Laham, A. (2007). Do entrepreneurship programmes raise entrepreneurial intention of science and engineering students? The effect of learning, inspiration and resources. *Journal of Business venturing*, *22*(4), 566-591.

Syed, I., Butler, J. C., Smith, R. M., & Cao, X. (2020). From entrepreneurial passion to entrepreneurial intentions: The role of entrepreneurial passion, innovativeness, and curiosity in driving entrepreneurial intentions. *Personality and Individual differences*, *157*, 109758.

IMPACT OF COVID-19 ON REMITTANCES: AN ANALYSIS OF KERALA ECONOMY

Minu Sadasivan

Research Scholar, Department of Economics, The New College, Chennai

Abstract

Covid 19 had a severe impact on migrant population in the world. India having the largest migrant population in the world was greatly affected during the pandemic. Kerala experienced tremendous flow in return migrants during Covid and it was estimated to be 4 lakh and there was expected to be a loss of Rs 13000 crore annual remittances for the state. There were several issues faced by the return emigrants during Covid; loss of employment was an important concern of the state. Kerala Migration Survey 2021 that was conducted during the Covid period collected data from 1985 return emigrants (REM) covering 1871 households. The survey used CATI (Computer Assisted Telephonic Interviewing) Method which is broadly a non-probability sample. The paper uses KMS 2021 data to analyse the return emigration to Kerala during Covid-19 and tries to discuss remittances and causes for return emigration in the light of Covid. The return emigrants are classified into three categories which are normal return emigrants (NREM), disress return emigrants (DREM) and return to re-migrate (RREM). The paper looks at their characteristics, their reasons for return and remittances of return emigrants. The theories associated with return migration are studied in order to understand the nexus between remittances and return migration. The theoretical analysis along with the migration history of the state helps in the conceptual framework of migration and development discipline. As the state is known for migration to the Gulf and the growth of social sectors due to the external remittances from the migrants, the role of state in protecting its emigrants is vital. The state has tried to rehabilitate the return migrants through several programmes. The present paper looks at the return emigrants and their choices of remittances and future plans in the light of Covid. Therefore, the role of return emigrants in the development of the state requires further research and policy level interventions.

Key Words: Return Emigrants (REM), Remittances, Covid-19, Kerala Economy

1. Introduction

The Covid pandemic that hit the globe shook the migrant population all over the world. The pandemic along with the economic crisis have created lots of concerns for the immigrants. The unexpected turn of events led to sudden policy responses including travel bans, lockdowns and social distancing which brought the economic activities to a standstill. This left the migrants with the choice of returning home from the foreign land. The migrants chose to return on an emergency so they were unprepared for such an event. They neither had a job back home nor were financially prepared. The return migrants were stigmatized as carriers of the virus (Rajan S. I., 2020). Indians represent 32 million in the diaspora and annually 25 lakh Indians migrate overseas, which is the highest in the world. Indian economy was greatly affected during the pandemic. This paper analyses the return migration to India by focusing on the state of Kerala. Kerala has a significant population of immigrants in foreign countries especially the Gulf countries (Zachariah, Kannan, & Rajan, 2002). The state economy receives huge foreign remittances from their NRIs and it results in investment in agriculture and non-farm economies and has helped to expand the consumption patterns of the people. Remittances varied according to educational levels of the migrants. The major end use of remittances was consumption; the other important uses were education, repayment of debt, construction and repair of buildings and bank deposits (Zachariah & Rajan, 2016). Kerala's economy is largely sustained by emigrant's remittances from gulf countries. Kerala has recorded fall in poverty during recent years of gulf-boom and the rate of wages has also gone up very high; since the timing of such improvements coincides with the period of remittances it is to be inferred that the remittances operate as the power behind such changes (Joseph, 2001). It is important to analyse the return migrants and their conditions after Covid pandemic. The migrants have several motifs behind their decision to migrate. Several studies show that remittances in several forms are one of the important economic motives. Probability to remit is not dominated by income alone; independent variables like age, education, gender, size of the household, employment and social dependency (Holst & Schrooten, 2006). Remittances can take different forms, but what is important is the motivation behind it. It is the mechanism with which they transfer a part of their gain from migration to their place of origin. Their motivation to remit may vary from supporting their family to buying property or other investment projects (Collier, Piracha, & Randazzo, 2011). Remittances play as an additional income to alleviate poverty, education of children, better health care, and financial security etc. (ibid). Since there are different types of migration like temporary, permanent, circular etc., what motivates the individual to remit still remains unclear.If the person decides to stay in the destination country permanently there might be a reduction in remittances, compared to a person who intends to return to home country. Temporary migrants remit regularly and consistently (Dustmann & Metres, 2010). The study also found that "the more likely a migrant is to return, the higher the probability of remitting for investment purposes" (ibid). Therefore, it can be argued that the type of migration also has an influence on the remittance of the individual and it is based on the intentions of the individual.

Migration from Kerala to the Gulf countries shows that end use of remittances is household consumption, followed by education, repayment of debt, construction and repairing of building and bank deposit (Zachariah, Mathew, & Rajan, 1999). The study also have categorized the migrant household depending on the value of the house and quality of housing. Based on this the present study aims at analyzing the post-covid impact of international migration. The state was able to achieve impressive socio-economic indicators and infrastructure, partly due to the remittances. Therefore, it is important to study the impact of covid on return emigrants and their investment pattern after the pandemic.

2. Theoretical background

It is not easy to thin down the migration process to a single theoretical understanding. Starting from the classical and neo-classical theory; it focuses on the wage differential factors as an important reason for migration. Later studies on labour market came up with theories like segmented labour market theory, social capital and migration network theory, human capital theory, new institutions theory and new economics of labour migration theory.

According to New Economics of Labour Migration (NELM) family was considered as an important unit of analysis for decision making. Stark and Lucas are important theoreticians who have kept family decisions as a determinant of migration decision. There are two types of economic models, the first focuses on migrant's utility function and on individual decision; the second focuses on intra-family contract while taking the migrant family as the decision making unit (Stark, 1995). The altruistic nature focuses on the utility of the relatives left behind. Remittances is measured based on income as well as the degree of altruism, which in turn uses the personal ties between remitter and the recipient. Unlike classical and neo-classical theories which focus on wage aspect of migration, it is the new economics of labour migration theory that mainly talks about the reasons for considering family as a unit. The neoclassical economic theory is focused mainly on the wage differences and considers migration as an individual decision to maximise their incomes. The neo-classical theorists completely ignored the fact that migrants are heterogeneous and are part of a community. It is important to look at the benefits accrued by the non-migrants in their families and communities. Under the NELM framework, the remittances that are brought by the migrants is used to diversify their livelihood means. This theory talks about the social aspect by identifying and acknowledging the fact that migrants belong to a community and the process of migration can bring out economic development and growth within their community. In this way they act as agents of change who bring about advancement. The return migrants are viewed as agencies of change that bring about social advancement and create incomes for non-migrants as well. Theorists Stark and Bloom stated that NELM makes it easy to manage multifaceted realities of the migration and development nexus. According to this theory, migration is not an individual decision, rather a collective decision that people take to bring up their family and community to a better position.

As per this theory, they use migrants as agencies of change who will bring about social advancement and betterment in their communities of origin. "New economics of labour migration theory regards migration as a family decision, aiming at minimizing the risks and overcoming temporary financial constraints. The dual work market theory and the global systems theory ignore, in general, the processes of adopting the decision to migrate on a micro level, focusing, in return, on the forces that act on a larger scale. It is not exclusively the individual that decides about migration. Rather, decisions are taken in the context of the family and the household, and migration is seen as a form of port-folio diversification by families" (Stark, 1991). He argues that, "wider social entities have to be taken into account while migration decision is made" (ibid). When poor families have insufficient income, they sent only one member to work outside, so they sent remittances which will have a positive impact on the sending economy. This income differences acts as an icentive to sent more people to other localities; it can be argued that migration will be higher in those areas which experience higher income inequality. The migrants who return brigs social change and transformation in the societies.

NELM theory has highlighted the need to focus on migration not just as a labour market phenomenon but have also tried to incorporate non labour market aspects as well into the analysis. It has tried to locate migration process within a wider framework of not just labour market but also other forces that act in line with the migration decision making. This holistic approach has helped in the betterment of understanding and studying the migration process from different viewpoints. This theory gives a pluralist view on migration and development. They view return migration as a positive phenomenon as migration is on a temporary basis and the duration of their stay outside their native land is based on the need of the household in terms of their savings, purchasing power, and insurance. When they are able to meet those requirements, they prefer to move back. It can be understood from this analysis that, as per the new economics of migration "return migration goes beyond a response to negative wage differential" (Stark, 1991). Whereas, neo-classical theory views return migration as a failure; therefore NELM theory can also be used to analyse return migration in the light of Covid-19. It is in the backdrop of this undersanding that the present paper further proceeds with the analysis and interpretation of Covid-retun emigrants.

3. Objectives

The main objective of the paper is to look at the return migration pattern in Kerala during Covid-19 and thereby analyse the investment pattern of return emigrants.

4. Methodology

The paper uses Kerala Migration Survey 2021 data for analysis and interpretation. KMS 2021 is conducted by Centre for Development Studies (CDS), Trivandrum as part of a Research Program on International Migration and International Institute of Migration and Development (IIMAD). The survey used Computer Assisted Telephonic Interviewing (CATI) Method. The survey was conducted from January to May 2021 on a sample size of 1985 REM (return migrants) from 1871 households. The sample was randomly drawn from a list of expatriates who returned to Kerala between April 2020 and November 2020 from any international destination. The sample is not weighted against the population of the district, and hence lacks representation, and is broadly a non-probability sample.

5. Findings and Discussion

5.1 Types of REM

The return migrants are classified into three categories depending on primary reasons for return. They are NREM (Normal Return Emigrants), DREM (Distress Return Emigrants) and RREM (Returned to Re-emigrate). The normal return emigrants are those who could have returned as per their plan but the date was advanced due to the pandemic. The distress return emigrants are those who were affected by the pandemic and were forced to return.

Table 1: Primary Reason for Return by REM Type

Sl No.	Primary Reason for Return	NREM	DREM	RREM	Others	Total
1	To Retire	28	0	0	0	28
2	Missed Family	29	0	0	0	29
3	Care for Elderly	11	0	0	0	11
4	Accomplished Work	13	0	0	0	13
5	Prefer to Work in Kerala	13	0	0	0	13
6	Lost Job/Laid off	0	955	0	0	955
7	Illness/Accident	0	70	0	0	70
8	Expiry of Contract	0	89	0	0	89
9	Scared due to Covid-19	0	461	0	0	461
10	Compulsory Expatriation	0	36	0	0	36
11	Low Wages	0	58	0	0	58
12	Poor Working Conditions	0	27	0	0	27
13	Nationalisation Policy	0	7	0	0	7
14	Visiting Visa Expired	0	20	0	0	20
15	Cancellation of Employment Visa	0	28	0	0	28
16	To Re-emigrate to another Destination or Same Destination for Different Job	0	0	18		18
17	Others (Specify)	0	0	0	122	122
	Total	94	1751	18	122	1985

Source: (Rajan S & Pattath, 2021)

Table 1 shows the different reasons for return migration and explains the categories of return emigrants. Among the returnees 4.7 percent are normal return emigrants, whereas 88.2 percent are distress return emigrants and only 6.1 percent have returned to re-emigrate. From this table, it can be analysed that majority of the Covid return emigrants have not expected this kind of a change in their migration journey. Reasons from no.5 to no.15 shows distress return emigrants and this change has resulted in the decisions of the migrants in several cases.

5.2 Demographic Characteristics of REM

The age pattern of migrants show in figure 1 explains that 32.6 percent of return emigrants are in the age group of 30 to 39 years followed by 24.3 percent in the group of 40 to 49 years.

Figure 1: Age of REM

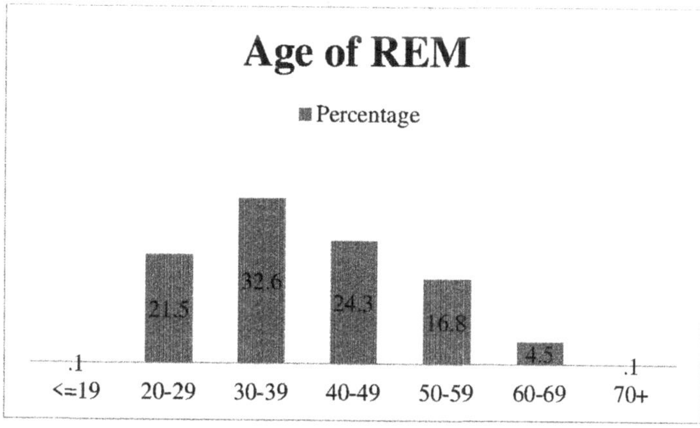

Source: KMS 2021

Categorizing the age of return migrants with the type of REM shows that, out of the DREM 32.4 percent are in the age group of 30 to 39 years; 25.3 percent between 40 to 49 years and 21.5 percent between 20 to 29 years. Table 2 shows the cross tabulation of age with the types of REM.

Table 2: Cross Tabulation of Age with Types of REM

Age group	Types of REM			Total
	NREM	DREM	RREM	
<= 19	0	1	0	1
20-29	13	339	49	401
30-39	28	507	77	612
40-49	20	399	38	457
50-59	29	251	36	316
60-69	12	65	8	85
70 +	1	0	1	2
Total	103	1562	209	1874

Source: KMS 2021

Majority of the return emigrants are in the category of distress return. Normal return emigrants are the oldest having average age of 45.8; youngest return emigrants are in RREM category having an average age of 34.8; and the younger category falls in distress return emigrants having an average age of 39.5 years (Rajan S & Pattath,

2021). With regard to Covid, the emigrants who returned felt that theirs' was an unplanned and unsatisfied return. The decision to have a permanent migration comes after fulfilling the migration requirements back home. Therefore, the younger population in the sample opted for re-migrate to other countries or the same countries to accomplish their needs.

Figure 2: Religion of REM in Percentage

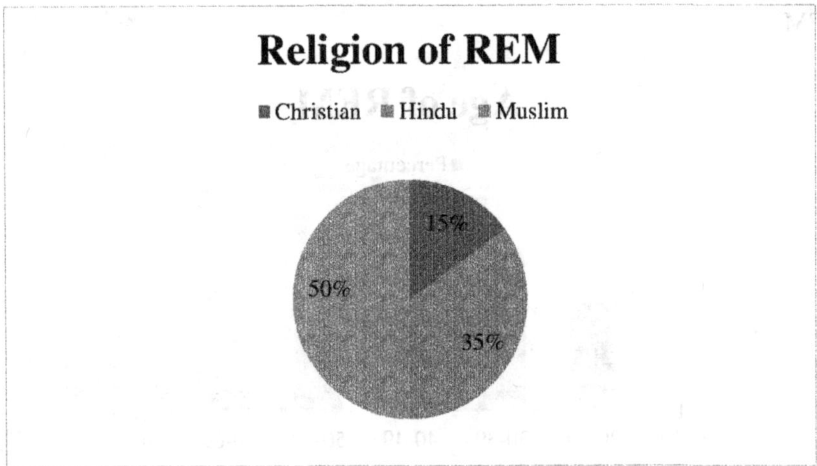

Source: (Rajan S & Pattath, 2021)

Figure 2 shows the religion of the sample, where 50 percent of the REM are from Muslim community followed by 35 percent Hindus and remaining 15 percent Christians. Majority of the return emigrants are male population (93%) and they are from rural locality (73%). 21 percent of REM are from Malappuram district; followed by 13 percent from Kozhikode which are in northern Kerala. Table 3 shows the destination countries of return emigrants.

Table 3: Destination Countries of REM

Country	Frequency	Percentage
UAE	422	22.5
Bahrain	253	13.5
Kuwait	216	11.5
Oman	188	10
Qatar	156	8.3
Saudi Arabia	178	9.5

Source: KMS 2021

Table 3 explains that 22.5 percent of return emigrants are in UAE; 13.5 percent in Bahrain and 11.5 percent in Kuwait. Several studies have shown that Gulf countries are a major destination of Kerala migrants since the 90s (Zachariah, Kannan, & Rajan, 2002; Zachariah & Rajan, 2016; Zachariah, Mathew, & Rajan, 1999). These studies show that remittances from the nonresident Keralites have led to investment in Kerala economy in all sectors especially in manufacturing and construction sector.

6. Covid-19 and Remittances

Covid-19 affected the international migrants in Kerala; uncertainties in the form of job loss, decreased wages, lack of social protection led to large scale return migration. The return emigrants have been classified into three categories, normal return emigrants (REM), distress return emigrants (DREM) and returned to re-emigrate (RREM) which are discussed in the previous section. The data collected shows that 75 percent of them sent remittances before Covid-19; it was used for debt payment (30%), household expenses (25%), periodic investment (21%) and maintenance (12%) (Rajan S & Pattath, 2021). Figure 3 shows the categories into which remittances are sent by return migrants.

Figure 3: Remittances by Categories

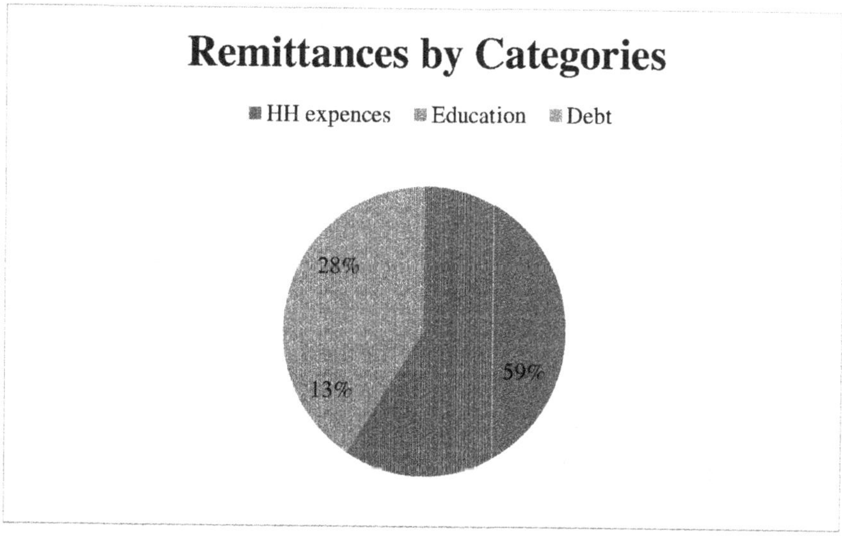

Source: KMS 2021

After the first lockdown, the data above shows that, remittances were made to household expenses, followed by repayment of debt and education. There are other categories like remittances in gold, cash, fixed deposit and land were also made.

A correlation test was done between the primary reasons for migration and total remittances. The output shows a significant relationship between the two variables. But a negative correlation is shown between the variables. Remittance is an important part of migration. The pre and post covid remittances of the return migrants show an increase; as majority of the return migrants are distress return, their way of responding to the unexpected event is by increasing the remittances. By this means, they are trying to secure their future by sending maximum and thereby keeping their future safe. The pre and post covid remittance demonstrates that there is an overall increase in monthly remittances which suggests that the remittances post lockdown increased (Rajan S & Pattath, 2021).

The monthly remittances have increased especially among the lower quartile; among DREM the percentage of remittances fell from 89.8 to 86 percent; among NREM, remittances increased from 68.6 to 97.3

percent (ibid). They were trying to send their accumulated savings to their home country.

The table 5 shows the cross tabulation of remittances with future plans of the REM pre-Covid and table 6 shows remittances with future plans of REM post-covid lockdown.

Table 5: Percentage of Pre-Covid Remittances and Future plan of Return Emigrants: Pre Covid Lockdown

Pre Covid Remittance	Start a New Business	Re-emigrate to get a new job	Re-emigrate to the same jobs before	Retired from work	Seek new job in Kerala	Others	Total
<10000	15.8	26.3	21.1	0.0	31.5	5.3	100
10000-19000	7.0	43.1	10.9	1.0	35.4	2.6	100
20000-28000	10.1	29.2	15.8	3.0	33.5	8.4	100
30000-40000	13.6	26.4	13.6	2.4	39.2	4.8	100
>40000	15.6	29.9	22.5	3.4	27.4	1.2	100
Total	12.6	32.1	17.9	2.7	31.4	3.3	100

Source: (Rajan S & Pattath, 2021)

Table 6: Percentage of Post-Covid Remittances and Future plan of Return Emigrants: Pre Covid Lockdown

Post Covid Remittance	Start a New Business	Re-emigrate to get a new job	Re-emigrate to the same jobs before	Retired from work	Seek new job in Kerala	Others	Total
<10000	20.0	20.0	20.0	0.0	40.0	0.0	100
10000-19000	11.8	45.1	7.8	2.0	33.3	0.0	100
20000-28000	19.7	40.9	10.6	1.5	25.8	1.5	100
30000-40000	17.2	37.9	13.8	0.0	31.1	0.0	100
>40000	17.0	27.7	19.8	2.3	31.1	2.1	100
Total	16.8	33.8	15.6	1.8	30.5	1.5	100

Source: (Rajan S & Pattath, 2021)

These two tables show the remittances of return migrants pre and post covid. A comparison of the table 5 and table 6 explains the different categories of future plans of the migrants and how the remittances were allotted for each options available. Those who have remitted to start a new business have increased overall from 12.6 percent to 16.8 percent; remittances and migration to the same jobs as before have decreased from 17.9 to 15.6 percent; the plan to re-emigrate to new job has increased from 32.1 to 33.8 percent. In the overall figures remittances show an increasing trend. The increase in the lower quartile of remittances shows a higher increase than that of the higher quartile. The data on the table is evident in a way that the future plan of the return migrants to remain Kerala and start a new venture is in a way more reliable to the migrants. The idea to re-integrate to Kerala economy and seek employment in Kerala is shown by 57 percent of return emigrants. The state has tried to rehabilitate the return migrants through several programmes. Therefore, the role of return emigrants in the development o the state requires further research and policy level interventions.

7. Conclusion

Emigrants are a major part of Kerala economy and for the overall development of the state. Migration flows were heavily affected during Covid-19. Among the majority of return emigrants, those who returned due to loss of jobs were the highest in percentage. Therefore, there is a huge responsibility lying with the state to reallocate these human resources into some productive ventures. It is the greatest challenge of the state government. There are several programmes introduced by the state to provide employment and other financial aid to the unemployed return emigrants. Covid-19 brought the concerns and issues of the migrants into limelight. There is a need to highlight the cost of migration and the implication of return migration. The mass return during the pandemic has thrown light on migration from different perspectives.Rehabilitation programmes and the need to strengthen the human resource of return migrants should be the focus of the state in the coming years.

REFERENCES

Collier, W., Piracha, M., & Randazzo, T. (2011). *Remittances and Return Migration.* Germany: Institute for the Study of Labour.

Dustmann, C., & Metres, J. (2010). Remittances and Temporary Migration. *Journal of Development Studies* , 62-70.

Holst, E., & Schrooten, M. (2006). *Migration and Money: What Determines Remittances? Evidence from Germany.* Berlin: German Institute for Economic Research.

Joseph, K. V. (2001). Factors and Patterns of Migration: The Kerala Experience. *Jornal of India School of Political Economy* , 55-72.

Rajan S, I., & Pattath, B. (2021). *Kerala Return Emigrant Survey 2021: What Next for Return Migrants of Kerala.* Trivandrum: Centre for Development Studies.

Rajan, I. S., & James, K. S. (2007). *Demographic Transition and Economic Development in Kerala: The Role of Emigration.* Kathmandu: South Asia Network of Economic Initiatives.

Rajan, S. I. (2020). Covid-19-led Migration Crisis: A Critique of Policies. *Economic and Political Weekly* , 13-16.

Stark, O. (1995). *Altruism and Beyond.* Cambridge: MIT Press.

Stark, O. (1991). *The Migration of Labour.* Oxford: Basil Blackwell Ltd.

Zachariah, A. C., & Rajan, I. (2016). Kerala Migration Study 2014. *Economic and Political Weekly* , 66-71.

Zachariah, K. C., Kannan, K. P., & Rajan, I. S. (2002). *Kerala's Gulf Connection: CDS Studies on International Labour Migration from Kerala State in India.* Trivandrum: Centre for Development Stdies.

Zachariah, K. C., Mathew, E. T., & Rajan, I. (1999). *Impact of Migration on Kerala's Economy and Society.* Thirvananthapuram: Centre for Development Studies.

Zachariah, K., Mathews, S., & Rajan, S. I. (2000). *Socio-Economic and Demographic Consequences of Migration in Kerala.* Thirvanathapuram: CDS Working Paper 303.

AGRO PERISHABLE EXPORTS IN POST PANDEMIC ERA: AN EVALUATION

Nahla Banu K
Research Scholar, PSMO College Tirurangadi
Nissar P
Research Supervisor, PSMO College Tirurangadi

Abstract

The COVID-19 epidemic has had unheard-of effects on the worldwide economy as well as terrible health effects and economic disruptions. The world's governments' restrictive policies have been blamed for a significant decline in global trade. Despite the government's priority of maintaining the main supply chains for necessities like food and medical supplies during the crisis, there have been multiple reported shipping and supply chain bottlenecks. Air cargo availability has been constrained by the cancellation of passenger flights related to travel bans, while urgent shipment of necessities has raised demand. This has led to price hikes for air cargo, which have had a substantial impact on their export performance. The purpose of this study was to investigate the post-pandemic patterns in agricultural exports in India.

Introduction

A number of diseases, such as the Spanish flu, Asian flu, Hong Kong flu, HIV/AIDS, SARS, Ebola, and swine flu, have had a substantial impact on agriculture, education, the economy, and human activities, such as leisure, shipping, health, fishing, mining, industry, and trade.(Mumtaz et al., 2021) The unique COVID-19 viral outbreak has expanded throughout the world, disrupting agricultural trade in China and the rest of the world in ways that have never been seen before.(Cao et al., 2021)However, there is a significant distinction between the COVID-19 pandemic in 2020 and the 1918 pandemic—this time, food scarcity is not a concern(LIN & ZHANG, 2020) While grain and oil exports maintained steady or even climbed during the pandemic, the typical agricultural firms in the survey experiencing lower exports, this suggests that crucial demand for staple foods(LIN & ZHANG, 2020). In addition to that, despite ongoing discussions about the consequences, some research indicate that exports of items like eggs and basics are not significantly impacted whereas exports of meat are negatively affected (Mallory, 2021).

Literature Background

In addition to having an adverse effect on people's health and quality of life, the current epidemic has also affected the supply chain and the world economy (Memon et al., 2021) Many small businesses have been forced to close permanently as a result of lockdowns and restrictions implemented by the government to stop the spread of disease. (Kalogiannidis, 2020) Due to COVID 19, workers' freedom of movement was restricted, consumer demand changed, food production facilities were closed, food policies were regulated, and the food supply chain was under financial strain (Aday & Aday, 2020) According to the analysis, global exports of services would decline significantly in the second quarter of 2020, by over 10%. Financial, travel, and transportation industries have been worst damaged (Veeramani & Anam, 2021) In relation to beverages to the COVID-19 effect, the rate of annual revenue growth and total profit growth further decreased to 2.6% and 8.9%, respectively, in 2020. (Memon et The majority of farmers also expressed worry that COVID-19 would make it more challenging for them to regularly get adequate food for their household (82.5%); that the markets where they buy food will either be closed or seriously disrupted (79.5%)(Middendorf et al., 2021);_(LIN & ZHANG, 2020) During the pandemic, there was a considerable surge in the export of medical herbs. Exports of goods including horticulture products and edible fungi, however, dramatically declined. The impact of COVID-19 on smaller businesses was generally more severe than on bigger businesses. Susceptibility varies depending on an entity's size, religion, or gender; for instance, women, small firms, and black entrepreneurs faced significant challenges. (21, 22) (Haqiqi & Bahalou Horeh, 2021) (Lopez-Ridaura et al., 2021). Middendorf et al., 2021b)

Research Problem

More than 200 nations and areas worldwide have adopted the COVID-19. However, the agricultural supply chain in the control area suffered greatly. In terms of global epidemic prevention, all countries are strengthening their border blockades, protecting their own food demand, and strict import and export quarantine measures have significantly reduced the spread of the epidemic, hence devastated the economy across the globe. China, as the first country to fight the epidemic, took measures such as social isolation, regional blockade, and traffic control, which is followed by many other nations leads temporary stoppage of international freight movement.

Whether the country is resilient to the virus spread?

Figure 1

	2019-20			2020-21			2021-22	
Importing Countries	**Qty**	**Rs. Crore**	**Importing Countries**	**Qty**	**Rs. Crore**	**Importing Countries**	**Qty**	**Rs. Crore**
Netherland	201.96	148.39	U S A	867.53	140.76	Netherland	161.96	122.58

U S A	671.79	118.89	Netherland	165.79	138.75	U S A	329.33	120.73
Bangladesh	6951.18	78.42	Bangladesh	8631.14	119.13	Bangladesh	3903.77	84.28
Thailand	157.93	48.15	UAE	2594.35	48.17	Thailand	103.96	36.84
Pakistan	1517.22	31.35	Japan	131.53	27.5	UAE	1926.31	32.19
Japan	146.67	28.05	Korea	281.79	25.9	Japan	115.65	29.43
Iran	290.41	23.95	Thailand	64.17	25.86	Korea	95.05	24.44
Korea	154.97	20.72	Kenya	140.35	23.82	France	43.84	23.89
France	39.36	16.89	France	40.2	19.59	Kenya	90.87	23.62
Malaysia	212.65	14.34	Vietnam Soc Rep	467.78	18.49	Nepal	1205.68	20.72

Source: DGCI

Figure 2

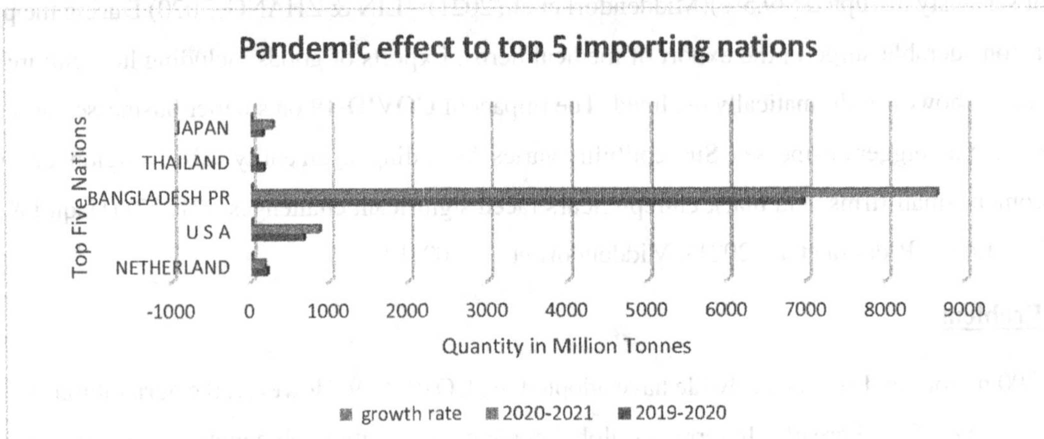

Source: DGCIS

India has enormous opportunities of international trade as the country is rich in production of agriculturalcommodities.Netahrland,USA,Bangladesh,Thailand,Pakistan,Japan,Iran,Korea,France,Malasia are the top 10 importing nations which are highly relied upon Indian cultivation. India exported 6951(million tonnes) worth rupees 78.42 (crores) to Bangladesh, where the country stands top importing nations. Despite the international restrictions in 2020-2021 as part of prevention of virus spread the country reported a hike in export volume approximately 8630 (Million tonnes). However, a fall in quantity of exports reported in the year 2021-2022 even if the nations across the globes remove bans. After Bangladesh, Pakistan stands the second position, however the nation was too responsive to the covid effect.

India's exports stagnated during the first &second phases of covid pandemic .the nation's export in 2019- 2020 to Netherland is 201 million tonnes, gradually total freight volume declined to165 million tonnes in 2020-

2021,while 2021-2022 export again declined 161 tonnage. Same trend also shows in the exports to United States of America in the post pandemic era, however a during 2020-2021 massive hike been reported. Bangladesh is the largest importer of agricultural products from India, which also reveals a positive trend amid the peak period of corona virus, however -55 % decline reported during 2021-2022.export towards Thailand shows a steep fall approximately 59%,hence shown a hike about 62 % in the post Covid era.

Conclusion and Discussions

The export volume to the top importing nations of the country indicates that there was a devastating trend at the beginning of the outbreak, but a massive rise in demand for Indian agricultural products on the global market occurred at the second quarter of 2020.market leaders continues their operations during India exports mainly agricultural products, such as fruits and vegetables, which are highly time sensitive and highly perishable. As a result, air shipment is highly relied on in order to ensure faster movement of goods to overseas markets. It is possible for the market leaders to chart flights and enjoy the benefits of large-scale operations by producing huge quantities. This resulted in small entrepreneurs struggling to survive on the market and incurring excessive freight charges. One of the major challenges faced by exporters is the airline's charges remaining the same as during the pandemic. In addition, the government plans to discontinue the 18% GST exemption on airfreight on October 1, 2022.

REFERENCES

Cao, L., Li, T., Wang, R., & Zhu, J. (2021). Impact of COVID-19 on China's agricultural trade. *China Agricultural Economic Review*, *13*(1), 1–21. https://doi.org/10.1108/CAER-05-2020-0079

Kalogiannidis, S. (2020). *Investigation of the process of redesigning the development identity of local self-government units, in terms of causes, content and effectiveness: A case study of the Greek Regional Unit Kozani View project NATIONAL CIVIL PROTECTION TRAINING CENTER View project Covid Impact on Small Business*. https://doi.org/10.23958/ijssei/vol06-i12/257

LIN, B. xi, & ZHANG, Y. Y. (2020). Impact of the COVID-19 pandemic on agricultural exports. *Journal of Integrative Agriculture*, *19*(12), 2937–2945. https://doi.org/10.1016/S2095-3119(20)63430-X

Middendorf, B. J., Faye, A., Middendorf, G., Stewart, Z. P., Jha, P. K., & Prasad, P. V. V. (2021). Smallholder farmer perceptions about the impact of COVID-19 on agriculture and livelihoods in Senegal. *Agricultural Systems*, *190*(September 2020), 103108. https://doi.org/10.1016/j.agsy.2021.103108

Mumtaz, M., Hussain, N., Baqar, Z., Anwar, S., & Bilal, M. (2021). Deciphering the impact of novel coronavirus pandemic on agricultural sustainability, food security, and socio-economic sectors—a review. *Environmental Science and Pollution Research*, *28*(36), 49410–49424. https://doi.org/10.1007/s11356-021-15728-y

COVID 19 PANDEMIC AND SOCIAL POLICY: IMPACT ON MIGRANT WORKERS IN KERALA

Shinu

Junior Research Fellow, Department of Commerce and Management Studies, PSMO College

Munavver Azeem Mullappallykayamkulath

Assistant Professor & Research Supervisor, Department of Commerce and Management Studies, PSMO College

ABSTRACT

In response to the COVID-19 outbreak, India declared a national lockdown on March 24th, 2020, leaving millions of migrant workers stranded in their final destinations. The COVID-19 pandemic has had a significant impact on migrants in the state of Kerala, India. Migrants in Kerala, who are often low-paid workers in sectors such as construction, agriculture, and domestic work, have been disproportionately affected by the pandemic and the measures taken to contain it, such as lockdowns and travel restrictions. Many migrants have lost their jobs and have been unable to return to their home states due to the travel restrictions, leading to financial hardship and an inability to access basic necessities such as food and shelter. There have also been instances of discrimination and stigma against migrants in Kerala due to the misinformation and fear surrounding the spread of the virus. The government of Kerala has taken steps to address the challenges faced by migrants, including providing food and shelter to those in need and implementing measures to prevent the spread of the virus among the migrant population. And also implemented a variety of programmes for the inclusion of the workers and was able to effectively meet their demands all across the state-wide lockdown. This paper overviews the steps that the Kerala government has taken to address the situation and analyses the specific ways in which migrant workers of Kerala have been affected by the pandemic.

Keywords: COVID-19, Kerala, Migrants, Social Policy.

Junior Research Fellow, Department of Commerce and Management Studies, PSMO College), Tirurangadi. shinup.haridasan@gmail.com , 9539916199.

Assistant Professor & Research Supervisor, Department of Commerce and Management Studies, PSMO College (Affiliated to University of Calicut), Tirurangadi. munavverazeem@gmail.com, 9048676459.

INTRODUCTION

Interstate migrant workers' evacuation from different areas and subsequent return to their native lands provided many of the terrible sights of India's shutdown. The shutdown froze their employment and means of survival, so they trekked back to their home regions with luggage on their shoulders, kids in their arms, with barefooted

(Diwakar & Viswambaran, 2022) . During the initial stage of Coronavirus, primary worries for migrant workers included issues with unemployment and loss of income, food scarcity, paying the rent for a home, medical costs, worries about the wellbeing of their families (MoFHW)., 2020). The Indian Supreme Court directed the state and federal governments to intervene to meet the requirements of the trapped migrants after taking "suo motu" notice of their condition (Bhushan, 2021). Meanwhile, at the same time, Kerala, a small Indian state, rose up, made prompt measures, and successfully managed the situation.

In the month of January 2020, Kerala was the only state to identify and record COVID 19 instances in the nation, Kerala has also been a leader in putting different measures to control the spreading of Corona virus (Gulia & Kumar, 2020). Kerala at the time received recognition from around the world for its response to the outbreak (Diwakar & Viswambaran, 2022). The Kerala method is used by the Indian Council for Medical Research (ICMR) when developing screening and prevention methods, also the ICMR praised Kerala's strong health sector (PTI, 2020). Kerala is the first Indian state to have passed legislation acknowledging and safeguarding the requirements of migrant workers, addressing to them as "guest workers" to lessen societal humiliation (Shibu, 2020). To determine how many laborers are departing or coming Kerala, the state of Kerala performed its own migration study (Irudaya Rajan & Zachariah, 2020). The establishment of social programmes for migrant workers arriving in Kerala is reflected in its strong IMPEX (interstate migrant policy index) rating (Aggarwal et al., 2020).

Table 1 : The Interstate Migrant Policy Index, 2019

State	Interstate Migration Census (2011 a)	IMPEX Score: Overall (out of 100)	IMPEX Score: Social Benefits (out of 100)
Kerala	0.6 million	63	54
Maharashtra	9 million	44	50
Uttar Pradesh	4.06 million	35	0
Gujarat	3.9 million	35	22

Source https://indianmigrationnow.org/impex-2019/

THE IMPACT OF COVID-19 PANDEMIC

Impact on working and living condition.

Migrant workers experienced a variety of social, financial and mental issues as a result of the lockdown, including feeling of rejection, monetary loss, worry about potential earnings, insecurity about one's wellness, and physical and social separation throughout the shutdown time (Khanna, 2020).

91% of migrant laborers experienced high rate of unemployment at the time of initial shutdown (March to May 2020), when those migrant laborers lost their employment, they were forced to deal with a severe economic problem (Diwakar & Viswambaran, 2022). During the lockdown time, the contract laborers received their partial salaries; however, the remaining independent laborers did not get any monetary help, so their families sent cash to them (Peter Anjana, 2021). During the shutdown, period 15% of the migrant laborers reported they had no access to three times meals daily, and 11% claimed the meals was unhealthy (Diwakar & Viswambaran, 2022). Inadequate dwelling, cleaning, power, kitchen gas, and water amenities are also the crisis faced by migrant workers during lockdown (Rao, Narain, Chakraborty, Arundhita Bhanjdeo, et al., 2020). Obtaining assistance from authorities proved difficult for migrant workers because of administrative restrictions (Rao, Narain, Chakraborty, Bhanjdeo, et al., 2020).

Impact on housing and accommodation.

The contract did not cover the rent for the migrant worker's residence or cancel it, they thus had trouble making the rent payments on the residence and migrants also admitted that they found it challenging to satisfy their basic demands, including covering their phone recharging and power cost (Diwakar & Viswambaran, 2022). The purpose of the lockdown period was to implement "social separation" in order to stop the transmission of the virus. But in their impermanent, congested dwellings, the migratory workers were unable to meet those requirements (Sengupta Sohini & Jha Manish, 2020).

Impact on healthcare

For migratory laborers, the availability of medical facilities and use of medical services are major concerns. Despite being exposed to several health risks due to their employment in the informal sector, they have not been protected by any state welfare programmes (Diwakar & Viswambaran, 2022). If migrant workers are identified as Covid Positive, they fear harassment and humiliation. Therefore, they are reluctant to go for covid checking, which is accompanied by quarantine (Peter Anjana, 2021). But Kerala offers greater access to medical facilities and the option to purchase medications throughout shutdown span. Only approximately 2.3% of people had trouble paying for medications, and 3% had trouble finding physicians to examine for illnesses. Otherwise, getting and using medical services in Kerala was not problematic for the rest 97% migrants (Diwakar & Viswambaran, 2022).

KERALA GOVERNMENT RESPONSES TO COVID-19 PANDEMIC- POLICY INTERVENTION

The migrant workers were seriously affected by the lockdown that was implemented on March 25, 2020, to prevent the transmission of the COVID-19 illness (Peter et al., 2020). Although the nation as a whole saw such a hardship of migrant workers and the government fought to control the catastrophe, the condition in Kerala was significantly improved one (Peter et al., 2020). In this part of the paper, the researcher look at Kerala's reaction to the problems encountered by migrant workers.

The National Health Mission of the Government of Kerala, in collaboration with NGOs, created and broadcast COVID precautionary information in various translations in just 15 days of the detection of the initial COVID-19 situation in India (Gazette, 2020). The government has removed the suffering of migrant workers by the state-level policy initiatives, it has recorded and engaged in supplying meals and other basic amenities to around 4.3 lakhs of migrants in Kerala, in spite the approximate interstate migrant laborers in 2019 totalling more than 3 million (Malhotra, 2022).

Under The Department of Local Self-Government (LSGD), Deprivation of Liberty Safeguards (DOLS), and the Department of Revenue, the Civil Supplies Department gave grains and atta to migrant labourers (Local Self Government, 2020). The state's pregnant women and migrant workers, in addition to the students who enlisted in anganwadis, received the milk gathered from producers that was not pasteurised (Peter et al., 2020). According to the State Planning Board's Economic Review 2020, no migrant workers were denied access to necessary facilities thanks to the Labour Department's action (Kerala State Planning Board, 2022). To supply migrant workers with varied amenities, particularly in Covid scenarios, a comprehensive record of migrant laborers in the State and their inflow and outflow is necessary and to handle all of the migrant workers' needs, including job, housing, and other amenities, the department is creating a smartphone apps, the authorities can assure services for them, including immunization and quarantine centres during outbreaks, with the help of this reliable statistics on migrant laborers in the state (Kerala State Planning Board, 2022). With the assistance of the District administration, efforts were made to create distinct CFLTCs (Covid First Line Treatment Centres) that are only for migrant laborers (Kerala State Planning Board, 2022). In response to the Government of India's declaration of the Shramik special railways, the departments collaborated to examine migrant workers for COVID and help them to go back to their homeland. The vehicles of the Kerala Police and the KSRTC transported authorized laborers to different transportation hub (Peter et al., 2020). During March to June 2020, 26 trains transported a total of 10,425 migrant workers back to their home land (Bava et al., 2021).

Table 2: State wise distribution of migrant labourers

State	Total
West Bengal	7426
Bihar	1601
Odisha	159
Jharkhand	432
Chhattisgarh	47
Assam	449
Uttar Pradesh	225
Rajasthan	22
Madhya Pradesh	29
Uttarakhand	21
Others	14
Total	**10,425**

Source: Revenue and Labour Departments

Numerous migrant hostels have been established throughout the state with the purpose of housing the homeless migrant workers, relocating migrant workers residing in congested areas, and isolating the sick migrant workers (Bava et al., 2021).

To provide the migrant labourers with improved services, camps were established. There were four various kinds of migrant workers camps built. Camps run by District Administration- Under these cooked meals were given to the migrants at this location by Kudumbashree utilizing their own money and the community kitchen maintained by the LSGD with the assistance of volunteer organizations. Camps run by Employer/Contractor- Shelters scattered in rented buildings/converted as camps, Shelters scattered; for workers not willing to join camps (Kerala State Planning Board, 2022).

CONCLUSION

This paper has overviewed the ways in which migrant workers of Kerala have been affected by the Covid pandemic and the steps that the Kerala government has taken to address migrants suffering during the national lockdown. Migrant labourers in Kerala have been significantly impacted by the COVID-19 outbreak. Economic crisis has resulted from numerous migrants losing their employment or having their earnings severely diminished. Migrants have found it challenging to go back to their native states as a result of border restrictions and rigorous lockdown regulations. Many migrants have been left trapped in Kerala as a result, without availability of accommodation, food, or medical assistance. The state government has established a number of social policies to aid migrants during the Covid-19, such as giving food and housing, but the severity of the situation has hampered the impact of these initiatives. The pandemic has, in general, brought into focus the demand for an improved social safety for migrants and other disadvantaged people in Kerala and other regions of India.

REFERENCES

(MoFHW)., M. of H. and F. W. (2020). *PSYCHOSOCIAL ISSUES AMONG MIGRANTS DURING COVID-19*. 1–2. https://www.ptonline.com/articles/how-to-get-better-mfi-results

Aggarwal, V., Solano, G., Singh, P., & Singh, S. (2020). The Integration of Interstate Migrants in India: A 7 State Policy Evaluation. *International Migration*, *58*(5), 144–163. https://doi.org/10.1111/IMIG.12701

Bava, N., Sreekumar, S., Mathew, G., Sushan, A., Sheeja, A., & Parvathy, P. (2021). Strategies for COVID-19 control among migrant labourers in a developing country setting: Pathanamthitta model from Kerala. *Journal of Family Medicine and Primary Care*, *10*(6), 2342. https://doi.org/10.4103/jfmpc.jfmpc_2357_20

Bhushan, A. (2021). *Reportable IN THE SUPREME COURT OF INDIA CIVIL ORIGINAL JURISDICTION SUO MOTU WRIT PETITION (CIVIL) NO.6 OF 2020 IN RE: PROBLEMS AND MISERIES OF MIGRANT LABOURERS With Writ Petition (C) No.916 of 2020 Bandhua Mukti Morcha ...Petitioner Versus Union of India. 6.*

Diwakar, D. G., & Viswambaran, V. (2022). Brandeis University, Center for Global Development and Sustainability Impact of Covid-19 on Livelihood and Health Experiences of Migrant Labourers in Kerala, India. *Source: CASTE: A Global Journal on Social Exclusion*, *3*(2), 299–318. https://doi.org/10.2307/48695953

Gazette, K. (2020). േകരള ഗസറ്. *2103*, 1–3.

Gulia, K. K., & Kumar, V. M. (2020). Reverse quarantine in Kerala: managing the 2019 novel coronavirus in a state with a relatively large elderly population. *Psychogeriatrics*, *20*(5), 794–795. https://doi.org/10.1111/psyg.12582

Irudaya Rajan, S., & Zachariah, K. C. (2020). New evidences from the Kerala Migration Survey, 2018. In *Economic and Political Weekly* (Vol. 55, Issue 4, pp. 41–49).

Kerala State Planning Board. (2022). *ECONOMIC REVIEW 2020 GOVERNMENT OF KERALA*. www.cdit.org

Khanna, A. (2020). Impact of Migration of Labour Force due to Global COVID-19 Pandemic with Reference to India. *Journal of Health Management*, *22*(2), 181–191. https://doi.org/10.1177/0972063420935542

Local Self Government, G. (2020). *COVID 19- PREVENTIVE MEASURES GUIDE FOR LOCAL SELF GOVERNMENTS*.

Malhotra, A. (2022). *partition filed by the appellant herein, claiming 1/5th share in the suit properties. 1. 6659*, 1–51.

Peter Anjana. (2021). *A study on impact of Covid-19 pandemic among migrant workers in Kerala*. https://www.google.co.in/books/edition/COVID_19_and_Migrant_Health/leI_EAAAQBAJ?hl=en&gbpv=1&dq=problems+of+migrant+workers+during+covid+in+kerala&pg=PA68&printsec=frontcover

Peter, B., Sanghvi, S., & Narendran, V. (2020). Inclusion of Interstate Migrant Workers in Kerala and Lessons for India. *Indian Journal of Labour Economics*, *63*(4), 1065–1086. https://doi.org/10.1007/s41027-020-00292-9

Rao, N., Narain, N., Chakraborty, S., Arundhita Bhanjdeo, ·, Pattnaik, A., & Bhanjdeo, A. (2020). Destinations Matter: Social Policy and Migrant Workers in the Times of Covid. *The European Journal of Development Research*, *32*, 1639–1661. https://doi.org/10.1057/s41287-020-00326-4

Rao, N., Narain, N., Chakraborty, S., Bhanjdeo, A., & Pattnaik, A. (2020). Destinations Matter: Social Policy and Migrant Workers in the Times of Covid. *European Journal of Development Research*, *32*(5), 1639–1661. https://doi.org/10.1057/s41287-020-00326-4

Sengupta Sohini, & Jha Manish. (2020). Social Policy, COVID-19 and Impoverished Migrants: Challenges and Prospects in Locked Down India. *The International Journal of Community and Social Development*. https://sci-hub.st/10.1177/2516602620933715

Shibu, P.B. (2020). Kerala like Home, Not All Migrant Workers are in a Hurry to Leave. *The New Indian Express, 13 May.*

PERFORMANCE OF INITIAL PUBLIC OFFERINGS: A BIBLIOMETRIC AND LITERATURE REVIEW STUDY

Bhadrapriya V

Research Scholar,Department of Commerce and Management Studies ,Farook College (Autonomous),University of Calicut, Kozhikode,Kerala

Dr. T Mohamed Nishad

Associate Professor,Department of Commerce and Management Studies ,Farook College (Autonomous),University of Calicut, Kozhikode,Kerala

Abstract

This study aims to present a review and analysis of initial public offerings (IPOs) literature, both empirical and theoretical, given that IPOs have demonstrated tremendous growth in the past decade. This paper surveys the IPO literature published throughout 1997–2021 using a bibliometric review that involves qualitative and quantitative techniques. After that, some deep researches are conducted by bibliometric analysis such as Citation analysis, and Co- occurrence analysis (using VOS viewer software). In this study a total of 279 papers were selected and reviewed. The findings explain significant elements in the literature, including countries, institutions, journals, authors, articles, etc. Based on which further discussions are provided, including current challenges and possible directions. Finally, this paper explores the development trends of Initial Public Offerings, which offers an important reference for future research.

Keywords

Initial public offerings · Bibliometric analysis · VOS viewer software · IPO literature

1. Introduction

The decision of private firms to go public is one of the most fundamental decisions that the company faces in its life. It is the decision that changes the whole structure of the company. It is not surprising then that the IPO topic has attracted the attention of scholars, investors and decision makers. A vast number of studies have been conducted on the IPO topic, and it has been growing at faster pace in recent years. The past three decades have witnessed record growth in initial public offerings (IPOs). IPO growth in most developed, developing, and emerging markets are mainly driven by the securities market, which serves as its key economic component.

An Initial Public Offering (IPO) is the first run through when the stock of a privately owned business is offered to the general public. Initial public offerings are regularly given by similarly smaller and more youthful organizations looking for capital for development and broadening. These are additionally given when the enormous large organizations hope to turn out to be traded on an open market. They are discharged to fund-raise or capital for the organization. Other than making new monetary open doors for an organization, an IPO expands the company's public exposure also.

The IPO presents a less expensive fundraising choice than credit. Initial public offerings are a rewarding path for organizations to produce capital. They are generally chance free with regards to capital age. The investors in return for their cash get a portion of responsibility for the organization as in shares or regular stock. This proprietorship implies that if there should be an occurrence of misfortune, the cash got by the organization from the investors need not be payback to them since they are likewise, to a part, proprietors of the organization.

IPOs are deemed as indicators of the securities market's health. A series of successful IPO listings denotes a vibrant market and positive market sentiment, whereas a decline in IPO activities signals a bearish trend. Current IPO trends may drive or upset future offerings, explaining why market participants, the media, and regulators keep a close eye on IPO activities. IPO provides an alternative avenue for raising the needed capital for company growth and promoting sustainable economic development. Policymakers and researchers worldwide have a keen interest in this segment of the market. Such interest, along with unceasing IPO issuances, has led to the development of an extensive body of literature on this topic. Hence, this paper aims to thoroughly explore the published literature and contribute ideas for future studies.

Thorough research can drive existing efforts to enter a new developmental stage. This study demonstrates the current progress of IPO studies, with the more discernible aspects and future research directions. In capturing the richness of the IPO literature, bibliometric citation analysis and co - occurrence analysis is employed as the methods for analysing 279 articles published from the year 1997 to 2021.

The rest of this work is divided into seven parts. Section 2 has a background of the study, and Sect. 3 contains the Research methodology, Section 4 deals with data analysis and findings. Section 5 deals with conclusion, section 6 has limitations of present study. Section 7 has Authors contribution. Lastly section 8 has future avenues for the study.

Research Questions

This bibliometric study seeks to answer the following research questions:

- Which are the most influential journals and authors in the area of IPO performance?
- What is intellectual structure of the research community?
- What are the collaborative networks in the field of IPO performance?
- What are the most addressed issues in the recent work?

The above research questions translate into the following research objectives for the current paper.

- To elicit the trends or patterns in knowledge development in the area of performance of IPO's
- To investigate the knowledge structure and derive synthesis of knowledge.

II. Background of the study

New issuances, specifically IPOs or subsequent public offerings, are sold in the primary markets. An unlisted company's initial public offering is known as an IPO. ((Mehmood et al. 2020). According to research, it's important to control investor excitement during an IPO since investors have a propensity to overbid and mislead investments, which has a negative externality on the real economy (Veluvali 2019). According to the literature analysis, businesses use these markets in addition to raising cash to provide liquidity for investors and create a market for their shares (Ritter and Welch 2002). Consequently, there is a recognised need to build a strong regulatory framework for overseeing and directing IPO activities (Friedman and Grose 2006). Bibliometric citation analysis (Helbing 2019; Zhang et al. 2019) and content analysis (Kagzi and Guha 2018) are used as the methodologies for examining 2277 papers published from the years 1984 to 2020 in order to capture the depth of the IPO literature. Hence, there is a well-acknowledged need for establishing a solid regulatory framework for monitoring and channelling IPO activities (Friedman and Grose 2006). IPO provides an alternative avenue for raising the needed capital for company growth and promoting sustainable economic development.

III. Research Methodology

In fulfilling the research objectives, this study employed a systematic sample (articles) The highly comprehensive Scopus database was selected because it covers all top journals published since 1964. Data needed for this study were extracted after identifying and selecting an appropriate database. This was followed by running a search query using a right mix of multiple key words. Once the data set is established using the required inclusion and exclusion criteria, it is analysed with the help of software tools. Initially, a descriptive analysis of the data in terms of sources, documents and authors is conducted. This was followed by the bibliometric citation analysis and co - occurrence analysis for analysing 279 articles published from the year 1997 to 2021.

This current study applied two bibliometric citation analysis methods: (1) citation analysis and (2) co-occurrence analysis, The methodology is illustrated in detail in and Fig. 1.

Figure 1 Methodology

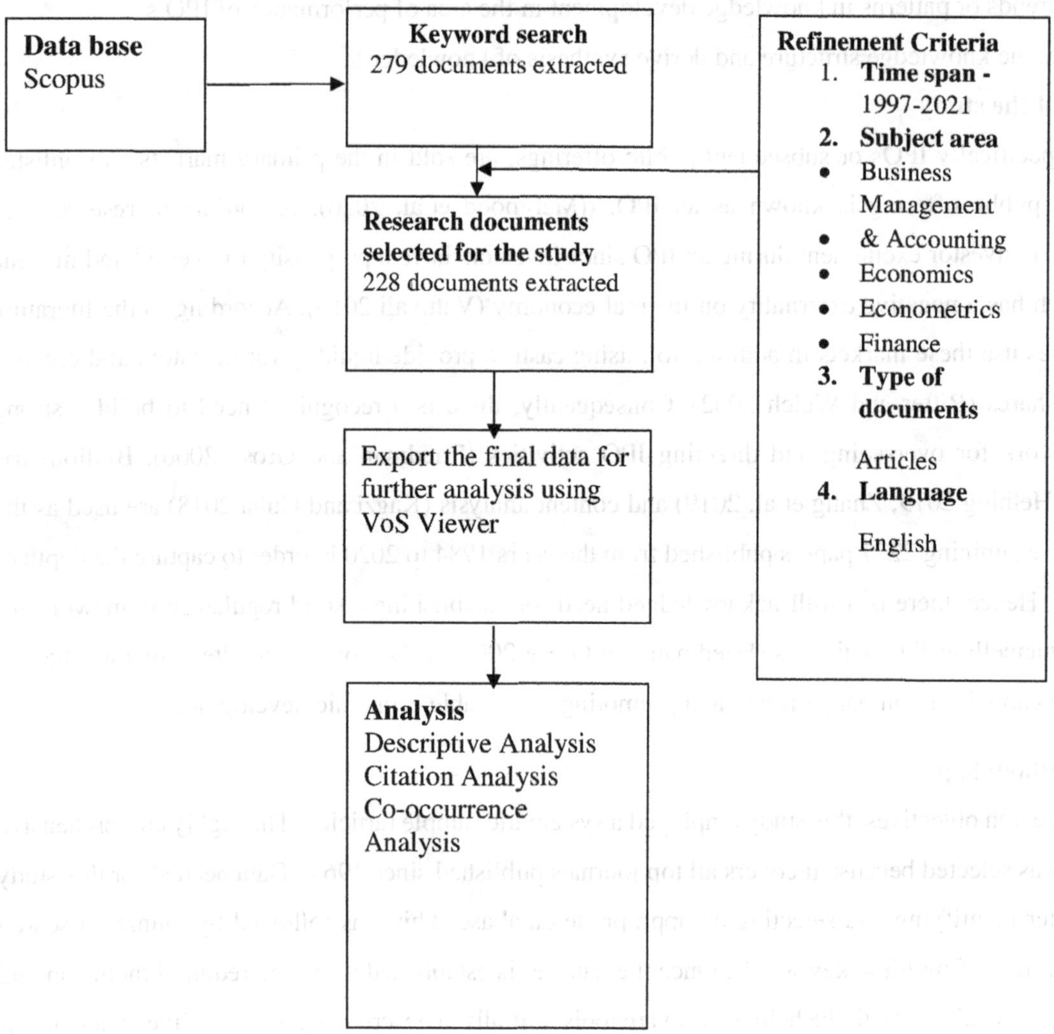

IV. Data Analysis and Findings

4.1 Descriptive analysis

This section on descriptive analysis discusses various dimensions undertaken for analysis. The current publication trend on IPOs was analysed using total publications based on the research trend by year, publishing activity by country, and publishing activity by journal. The data was calculated using the bibliographic data gathered from Scopus.

4.1.1 Research trend by year

Figure 2 shows the distribution of articles published from 1985 to 2021. 2021 is the most productive year for the number of IPO publications, i.e., 28. It can be seen that there has been an increasing interest in this topic mainly in the past decade (2010 to 2021). During 1997 to 2010, very few studies were conducted on IPO performance. The increasing number of studies conducted elucidate that IPO topic has attracted the attention of scholars, investors and decision makers.

Figure 2

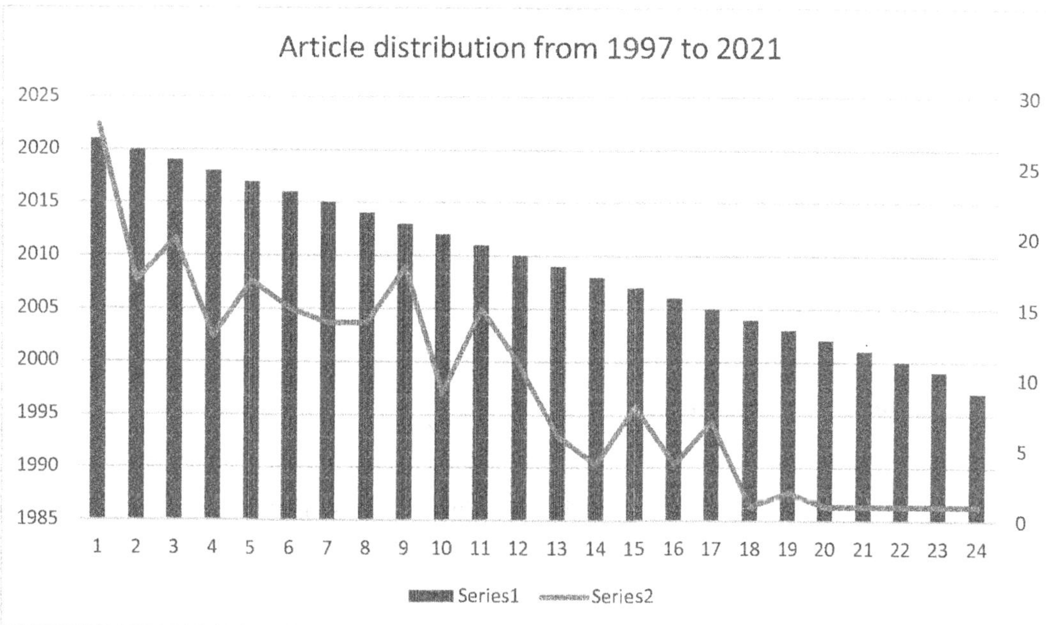

4.1.2 Journal of publication

The literature was analysed with respect to the journal of publication to identify important journals in this area. Results revealed that the data set of 228 is spread over 151 journals. 25 journals had two or more published articles, and these are shown in Figure 3. The remaining journals had only one published article each. The 50 journals comprise around 55 per cent of the journals covered in this study. It shows that the top two journals in terms of the number of research articles published are The Journal Of Corporate Finance and Review Of Quantitative Finance And Accounting with 8 and 7 articles, respectively.

Figure 3

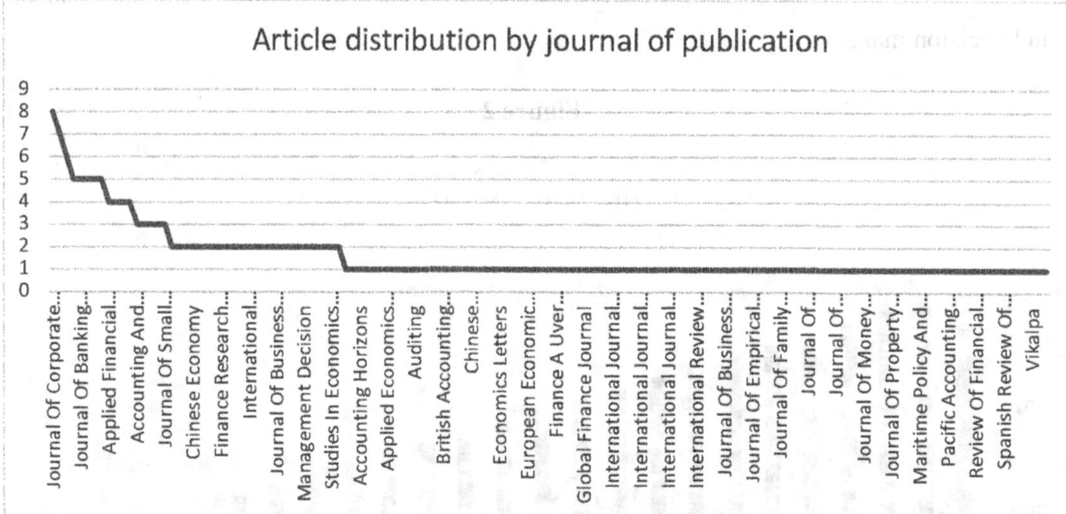

4.1.3 Country of sample data collection

Researchers have shown great interest in the IPO topic, as shown by the contributions from 49 countries. The top countries on IPO publications worldwide are led by the United States of America (US), China, the United Kingdom (UK), India, Hong Kong Australia, and Canada. Among the Asian countries, the top countries are China, and India.

Figure 4

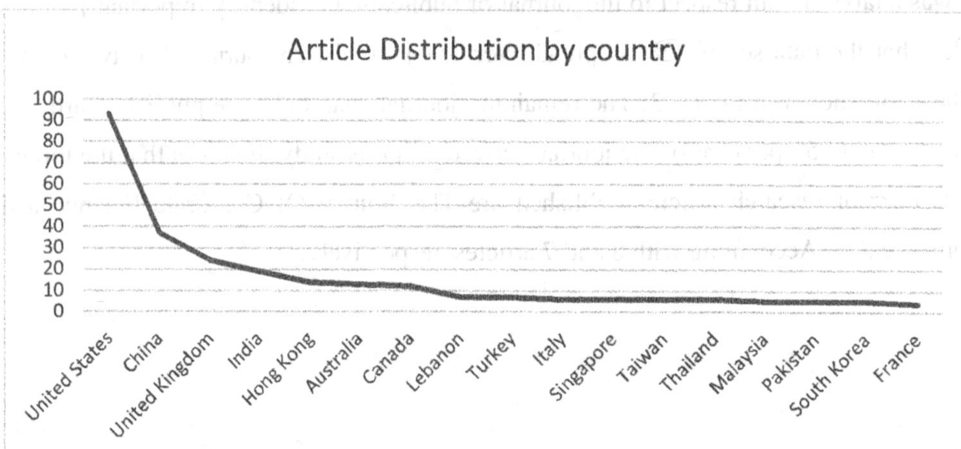

4.2 Citation Analysis; Top Authors and Organizations and Country: Table 1:

TC	Author	Documents	TC	organization	documents	TC	country	TP
1376	Zhang T	3	1345	city university of Hong Kong	1	2872	united states	94
279	Walters B. A	3	1345	the Chinese university of Hong Kong,	1	1553	Hong Kong	14
277	Thomas. J Chemmanur	3	552	Harvard business school, Boston,	1	565	China	37
163	Chahine. S	7	552	Harvard business school,	1	529	United Kingdom	24
160	Bell R.G	3	552	Kellogg grad. school of management,	1	470	Australia	13
160	Moore C. B	3	203	Australian school of business	1	378	Canada	12
136	Georgene M.	5	203	college of business and economics, Lehigh university,	1	326	Singapore	6
125	Tang J	4	203	U.S. securities and exchange commission,	1	215	Italy	6
124	Filatotchev. I	4	203	Weatherhead school of management,	1	171	Malaysia	5
122	Liu Q.	3	137	Florida state university,	1	163	Lebanon	7
85	Huang j.	3	137	Louisiana state university,	1	104	turkey	7
64	Gounopoulos.D	4	137	w. p. Carey school of business,	1	100	Germany	2
57	Chan K.C	5	61	economics university of Vienna, i	1	77	India	19
54	Wu. J	3	61	graduate school of management, university of Dallas,	1	73	France	4
36	Sahoo s.	3	61	M.J Neeley school of business, Texas Christian university,	1	72	Belgium	3
27	Ozdemir.O	3	61	sir john Cass business school, city university London,	1	66	Taiwan	6
21	Mcguinness P. B	3	5	business school, university of international business and economics, Beijing,	2	43	Thailand	6
20	Zhang y.	4	5	national institute of construction management and research, Pune, India	2	16	Saudi Arabia	2
19	Wang X.	3	1	school of business, Cessa	1	15	south Korea	5
7	Mumtaz M.Z	3	1	school of management, Universidad de los Andes, colombia	1	6	colombia	2

The top twenty authors are listed in Table 1. With 1376 citations and a maximum of 3 published documents, emerges as the most significant author in IPO performance .While the next followed by Walters B. A and Thomas. J Chemmanur with 279 citations and 277 citations and a maximum of 3 published documents.

In Table 1, the 20 organisations with the highest number of citations for articles on IPO performance are listed. The city university of Hong Kong& The Chinese university of Hong Kong is first with 1345 citations for a single document., Harvard business school, Boston, united states, Harvard business school, organizational behaviour unit, soldiers field park, Boston, &, Kellogg graduate school of management, north western university, is second on the list, with 552 citations and more than 10 organisations has more than 100 citations.

Ranking of the most cited countries is also shown in Table 1. The US has the highest number of widely cited authors (2872) on the topic of IPO performance. The Hong Kong (1553) is the second while China, United Kingdom, Australia, Canada among others, have also made significant contributions.

4.3 Keywords co-occurrence analysis

In Table 2 shown the most common keywords, their frequency, and their ranking in research papers on IPO performance These 10 keywords serve as a filter to help you better understand the common emerging trends in this research topic over time. They reflect the key themes in this research domain.

Table 2 Ranking Analysis of keywords co-occurrence

Rank	Keyword	Occurrences	Rank	Key word	Occurrences
1	IPO	36	6	Initial Public Offering (IPO)	9
2	Initial Public Offerings	34	7	long-run performance	8
3	Under-pricing	26	8	Earnings management	6
4	IPO performance	22	9	Information asymmetry	6
5	venture capital	14	10	IPO pricing	6

In Figure 5 is Presented the keyword co-occurrence network. The content in the chosen articles that is most pertinent to IPO is represented by these keywords. Additionally, these keywords make it easier to locate relevant articles when using search engines. According to the graph, the most popular search terms in the industry are Initial Public Offerings, Under-pricing, IPO performance, and venture capital

Figure 5: Keywords co-occurrence (created using VOS viewer)

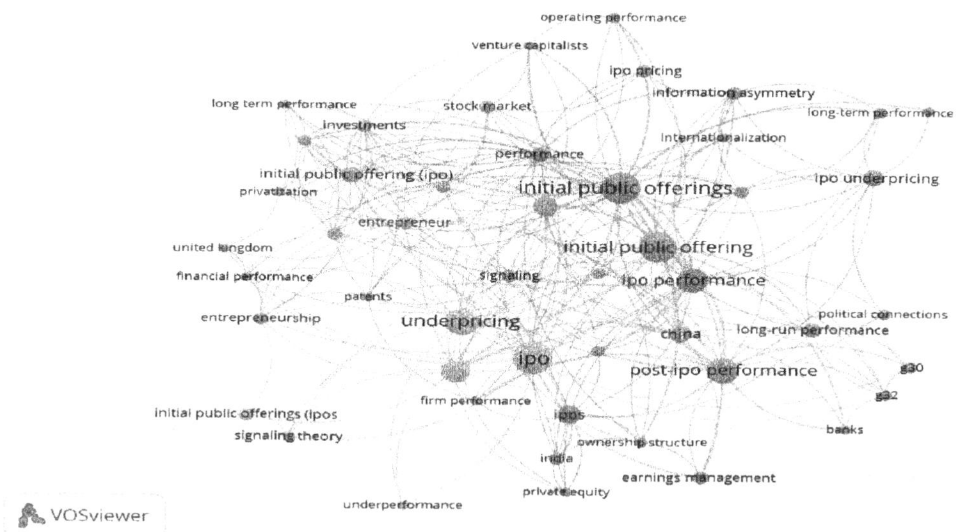

V. Conclusion

IPOs have been linked to the growth of the world financial and economic system. Declining IPO activity may have detrimental effects on global economies and societies at large. The IPO phenomenon thus involves not just technical finance but also managerial and economic conditions. More thorough theoretical frameworks should be developed by academics in the relevant domains to understand the IPO evolution and phenomenon. Researchers and authorities claim that IPO studies can improve the effectiveness of the stock market. The quality of a country is defined by the procedures that are being developed to increase the accountability of issuers, underwriters, and institutional investors. A country's quality is indicated by the transparency of its stock market.

This study uses both qualitative and quantitative methods to conduct a meta-literature review of studies that were released between the years 1997 and 2021. In this work, 279 articles from a single dataset with bibliometric analysis were reviewed. The data were derived from the Scopus database. The following methods were employed in the meta-literature review: (1) bibliometric citations to determine the literature's influential elements (2) co-occurrence analysis to determine the most prevalent keywords, their frequency, and their ranking in research papers.

This study adds to the field in a number of ways. It started by looking into the publication trends based on contributions from institutions, authors, and countries. By examining the mapping citations and co-authorship networks, it also determined which research and authors were the most influential. Third, to avoid stagnation and advance the profession, the study used co-occurrence analysis to map the most prevalent themes. Fourth, this study used bibliometric analysis to undertake a thorough and unbiased investigation of the literature.

6. Limitations

Contrarily, the researcher has some limitations, just like every other research paper. the one of our research paper's primary limitations due to Scopus being the only significant database that contains articles that have undergone peer review, this is one of our research paper's primary limitations. Second, the research's results depend heavily on the keywords that were selected; accordingly, changing the keywords might have led to different results.

7. Authors contribution

According to this study, there has been a noticeable increase in the amount of research on IPO Performance over the past years, and authors from a wide variety of nations have contributed. Networks of cooperation have been created as a result of greater integration among researchers to help close knowledge gaps. Additionally, similarities between the distinctive keywords of various articles in the field were discovered. These groups make it easier to identify contexts where various research philosophies overlap.

8. Avenues for future research

The purpose of this study was to identify gaps in literature on IPO Performance from 1997 to 2021. The researcher suggested that for expanding the articles' scope, a more robust research framework is needed for IPOs. For addressing various aspects relating to IPO Performance including the issues of underpricing, underperformance, IPO proceedings, strategic choices, performance outcomes, effectiveness, and monitoring, etc. there remains a need for broader studies on IPOs.

Most IPO studies concentrate on only one country. However, studies on developed countries are not generalizable to Asian countries due to institutional and socio-economic differences. Thus, more cross country and multiple countries are needed

A majority of IPO studies use datasets of companies from multiple sectors and offer cross-industry generalizations of the impact of IPOs. These generalizations are impractical due to the different industry characteristics Therefore, industry-specific studies are needed.

E-HRM ADOPTION STUDIES: PAST AND FUTURE RESEARCH

Archana PV

Assistant Professor, Department of Management Studies, LEAD College of Management, Dhoni, Palakkad

ABSTRACT

Profit and non-profit employers are constantly utilising electronic human resource management (e-HRM) systems. However, the field currently lacks solid theoretical frameworks that can be useful in addressing a key issue concerning the implementation of e-HRM systems, specifically to gain a better understanding of the factors influencing e-HRM system adoption. Through a review of the literature, the goal of this paper is to throw the groundwork for the development of a theoretical framework for the implementation of e-HRM systems and to create a conceptual model that reflects the nature of e-HRM system adoption. Using Crossan and Apaydin's systematic review procedure, this paper investigated 21 empirical papers on electronics human resource management and classified them into four characteristics that influence adoption: system and technology characteristics, organisational characteristics, user/individual characteristics, and environmental and contextual characteristics. Finally, the e-HRM adoption research framework is developed and discussed; avenues for future research are discussed.

***Keywords**: e-HRM, technology adoption, Technology Acceptance Model*

1. Introduction

Human resource management (HRM) practises in organisations are increasingly influenced by information systems (IS). During the last decade, the rapid development of the Internet and information technology has accelerated the adoption of electronic human resource management (hereafter called e-HRM).

According to Marler and Fisher (2013), e-HRM literature is still in its early stages when compared to general IT/IS literature or strategy literature, because early e-HRM studies began appearing in international publications around 1995. (Strohmeier, 2007).

While some organisations use e-HRM technology to improve HRM practises, and there is increased research interest in e-HRM, the field currently lacks sound theoretical frameworks that can be useful in addressing a key issue concerning the implementation of e-HRM systems, specifically to gain a better understanding of the factors influencing the adoption of e-HRM systems. Since academic interest and research in e-HRM adoption has grown, a review of the literature is required to identify the e-HRM adoption research trend as well as the literature gaps that will be useful for future research in order to improve understanding of e-HRM adoption.

Given the widespread use of e-HRM systems and the potential benefits and drawbacks associated with them, the primary goal of this article is to provide a review of the factors that influence e-HRM acceptance and adoption. The adoption and acceptance of information systems, in this case e-HRM systems, is determined by a variety of factors other than technology and advanced features. From a theoretical standpoint, the review may provide directions for e-HRM research by explaining the factors that influence e-HRM adoption, such as system and technology, organisational characteristics, user and individual characteristics, as well as environmental and contextual factors. From the perspective of managers and practitioners, the review also provides useful insights into how e-HRM can be implemented within organisations, where multifaceted and holistic factors drive IS adoption.

This literature review addresses the following research question: what factors influence e-HRM adoption in organisations, and how those factors are classified into four major groups or characteristics: system and technology, organisational, users/individuals, and environmental and contextual factors? The review included all technological applications and implementations related to Human Resource Management practises such as e-recruitment, e-selection, and e-training. Thus, the goal of this paper is to lay the groundwork for the development of a theoretical framework for the implementation of e-HRM systems, as well as to create a conceptual model that reflects the nature of e-HRM system acceptance and adoption. This paper will be presented in the following manner. The theoretical underpinnings and methodology used to compile empirical research from two popular academic databases via systematic literature review are explained in the following section. The results of the systematic literature review will then be presented, followed by a discussion and implications for practise and future research.

2. Literature Review

Electronic Human Resource Management (EHRM) is defined as the planning, implementation, and application of information technology for networking and supporting at least two individual or collective actors in the performance of HR activities (Strohmeier, 2007).

E-HRM can be used for a variety of HR-related tasks. It can be used for transactional activities (such as day-to-day transactions and record keeping); traditional HRM activities such as recruitment, selection, training, compensation, and performance management; and transformational activities that add value to the organisation, as well as managing HR across the entire employee lifecycle (Parry, 2011)

From a theoretical standpoint, organisations implement e-HRM to improve efficiency and service delivery, to increase the strategic orientation of the HR function, to improve standardisation and organisational image, and to empower managers. The primary outcomes of E-HRM are efficiency, service delivery and standardisation, relational outcomes, and potential improvements in organisational image (Parry & Tyson, 2011).

Previous research suggested that as electronic human resource management (e-HRM) systems become more widely used, e-HRM contributes to increasing the value of HR functions (e.g., Parry, 2011; Wahyudi & Park, 2014) and organisational innovation (Lin, 2011). However, the numerous positive outcomes of e-HRM implementation within organisations are not taken for granted. That is, e-HRM is just a technology that requires other factors to be successfully adopted and implemented.

Furthermore, in Human Resource practises (e.g., recruitment, selection, and performance appraisal), shifting from manual/traditional to electronic processing necessitates a thorough understanding of how e-HRM adoption and implementation work. People may be concerned about privacy invasion when submitting a job application via e-recruitment (Harris et al., 2003). In addition to that, e-HRM may reduce costs and speed up processes (Strohmeier, 2007), the technology requires installation, maintenance, and change costs, which forces organisations to consider the cost and benefits of the e-HRM system.

3. Research Method

As previously stated, a systematic literature review is conducted to identify and select relevant papers for this review. This study followed the procedure used by Crossan and Apaydin (2010) when conducting a systematic literature review on organisational innovation. The systematic literature review process will be described step by step, including planning, execution, and reporting.

3.1 Planning phase

The planning phase includes two major activities: defining the research objectives and identifying the key data source. To begin, the goal of the literature review is to identify and sketch a framework of all relevant factors influencing e-HRM adoption in organisations. Furthermore, two databases, ISI Web of Knowledge's Social Sciences Citation Index (SSCI) and Business Source Premier, were used to generate all relevant literature from 1995 to 2014.

3.2 Execution phase

The execution phase consists of data collection and organisation, as well as data processing and analysis. The process must identify preliminary selection criteria, such as keywords and search terms, and categorise the research papers/publications. The first step in the review process was to conduct a thorough search for scholarly peer-reviewed journal articles using two different search engines: EBSCO Business Source Premier and ISI Web of Knowledge. These two databases were used in this study to increase the number of available articles and increase the likelihood that the most relevant papers were included. The study only looked at papers published between 1995 and 2014.

Several keywords were used in the research to find relevant research papers. E-HRM researchers employ various e-HRM terminologies in their research, which generally refer to an information system-supported method of carrying out HR policies and practises (Strohmeier, 2007). They were used as keywords after researching the e-HRM terminologies used by e-HRM researchers.The keywords used in multi-searching in those two databases were combinations of e-HRM and synonyms/interchangeable terms (e-selection, e-recruitment, employee self-service systems, e-compensation, e-benefits, HR portal, virtual HR, web-based HR, e-learning HR, and Human Resources Information System), derivatives of adoption, derivatives of acceptance, and derivatives of diffusion. The process yielded an initial pool of 104 papers, including 39 from EBSCO Business Source Premier and 65 from ISI Web of Knowledge. Based on that initial pool, all of those papers were listed in a spreadsheet and then sorted to find duplicate papers with the same title. As a result, 48 papers had to be dropped: 13 from EBSCO Business Source Premier and 35 from ISI Web of Knowledge, leaving 56 articles for the rest of the paper.

Because those papers are from two different databases, the duplicate problem is still possible. As a result, the final screening involved combining all of those papers and removing duplicates as well as irrelevant papers, such as those that were not related to e-HRM adoption research, such as e-learning adoption and acceptance in medical school. Moreover, to keep the task manageable and to provide some assurance of quality research, only studies published in refereed international journals and articles based on empirical research were considered. Work published in books, research notes, open journals, conference proceedings, or working papers was excluded and deemed irrelevant. As a result, 35 papers had to be eliminated, leaving only 21 papers to be reviewed.

3.3 Reporting Phase

Following the reading of these articles, a summary of each paper was compiled in a table (see Appendix 2), which included the research problem, the main variables/hypotheses, the theoretical lenses/underpinning, research methods, and the findings/conclusion. The findings of the literature review will be synthesised and discussed in the following section.

4. Results and Discussion

Organizations can benefit from E-HRM systems. However, many e-HRM studies still lack theoretical consideration, and little is reported in the academic literature about the implementation of such systems (Tansley & Watson, 2000). As a result, the purpose of the literature review is to find an explanation of the various, multi-dimensional factors that contribute to e-HRM adoption in the organisation. Before going into that, the following section will go over the various theoretical underpinnings and methods used in the 21 research papers.

4.1 Theoretical Underpinning in e-HRM adoption research

The Technology Acceptance Model, proposed by Davis, is used in the majority of e-HRM adoption research. The Technology Acceptance Model is used as the theoretical lens in seven research papers.

It is not surprising given that the Technology Acceptance Model is the most widely used theory in e-HRM adoption research. Perceived usefulness and perceived ease of use have long been recognised as important factors in the success of new technology adoption, and a lack of user acceptance could stymie IS adoption (Davis, 1989). Several theories, including the Theory of Planned Behavior (TPB), the Unified Theory of Acceptance and Use of Technology (UTAUT) (Venkatesh et al., 2003), signalling theory, change management theory, and contingency theory, have been used in the e-HRM adoption research. Surprisingly, ten research papers do not specifically mention the theoretical theory they used. Based on the systematic literature review, each theory in the e-HRM adoption research will be discussed below.

The Theory of Planned Behavior (TPB) is one of the competing models in the acceptance of information technology. The Theory of Planned Behavior, in particular, extends the Theory of Reason Action (TRA) to predict human behaviour, which is then used to predict individual acceptance of Information Systems (IS). While the Theory of Planned Behavior only has two main constructs, attitude toward behaviour and subjective norm, it adds a construct, perceived behavioural control, as an additional determinant of intention and behaviour (Venkatesh et al., 2003). Lin (2010) investigates the impact of job seeker attitude, subjective norm, and perceived behavioural control on Theory of Planned Behavior (TPB) is one of competing models in IT accptance. The Theory of Planned Behavior, in particular, extends the Theory of Reason Action (TRA) to predict human behaviour, which is then used to predict individual acceptance of Information Systems (IS). While the Theory of Planned Behavior only has two main constructs, attitude toward behaviour and subjective norm, it adds a construct, perceived behavioural control, as an additional determinant of intention and behaviour (Venkatesh et al., 2003). Lin (2010) investigates the influence of job seeker attitude, subjective norm, and perceived behavioural control on the intention to use job search website using the Theory of Planned Behavior.

Despite its popularity in information system research, the Technology Acceptance Model has been criticised (Legris et al., 2003). In addition, the Unified Theory of Acceptance and Use of Technology (UTAUT) was developed to differentiate between intent to use and actual usage (Venkatesh et al., 2003). They contend that the intention to use will influence IS acceptance. This theory was used to investigate the effects of language standardisation on the acceptance and use of e-HRM systems (Heikkila & Smale, 2011).

The Technology Acceptance Model has been criticised despite its popularity in information system research (Legris et al., 2003). Furthermore, the Unified Theory of Acceptance and Use of Technology (UTAUT) was developed to distinguish between intent to use and actual usage (Venkatesh et al., 2003). They argue that the intention to use has an impact on IS acceptance. This theory was used to investigate the effects of language standardisation on e-HRM system acceptance and use (Heikkila & Smale, 2011).

Wahyudi and Park (2013) combine the Technology Acceptance Model with contingency theory as well. The contingency theory emphasises that outcome variables are determined by best fit and contextual factors. According to Wahyudi and Park's findings, the leadership style in organisations serves as a contextual factor in the adoption of e-HRM.

To investigate the Human Resources (HR) portal implementation, change management theory has been combined with the Technology Acceptance Model (Ruta, 2005). The process of implementing an HR portal is extremely complex. Employees interacted with people prior to the implementation of the HR portal, but after the implementation, employees must become acquainted with information technology and accept interaction with computers. Organizations must manage the change process well so that employees accept the HR portal and organisational change runs smoothly.

To summarise, the majority of theories used in adoption studies are one-sided and favour the positivism approach. Furthermore, the researchers used a single theory to investigate e-HRM adoption, despite the fact that few studies combine two types of theories, such as contingency theory and change management theory.

4.2. Research Methodology in e-HRM adoption research

Both quantitative and qualitative research methodologies are used in e-HRM studies. In particular, e-HRM adoption researchers employ a variety of research strategies, including mixed methods, action research, exploratory case studies, and survey research. Below, each research methodology will be described. Both quantitative and qualitative research methodologies are used in e-HRM studies. In particular, e-HRM adoption researchers employ a variety of research strategies, including mixed methods, action research, exploratory case studies, and survey research. Below, each research methodology will be described.

The most widely used research methodology in the study of e-HRM adoption is survey research. 13 research papers use survey research in this comprehensive evaluation of the literature. Because the theoretical basis of e-HRM is founded on psychology, such as the Theory of Rational Action, the Theory of Planned Behavior, the Technology Acceptance Model, or UTAUT, the researchers who study e-HRM primarily use this type of research methodology. Researchers in e-HRM analyse survey data to look for correlations and test any hypotheses between independent variables like perceived usefulness and perceived ease of use and dependent variables like intention to use and actual use. Additionally, in order to assess mediating variables or mediator variables that affect the relationship between independent variables and dependent variables, e-HRM researchers also create more complicated models.

Case studies and action research are some research methods that e-HRM researchers use from the qualitative research approach. Typically, they interview employees and users of the e-HRM system after doing their research in one or more organisations. To assist the data analysis, they additionally employed secondary data (e.g., Panayotopoulou et al., 2010). Finally, using within-case analysis and cross-case analysis, the data are examined and contrasted. In addition, mixed technique is rarely used by e-HRM researchers. Typically, they use questionnaires to perform survey research, which is subsequently followed by focus groups or interviews (e.g. Panayiotopoulos et al., 2007).

In conclusion, despite the fact that only a small number of studies used qualitative research, survey research constituted the majority of the e-HRM adoption research method. The best type of research is a survey. The Theory of Planned Behavior (TPB), the Technology Acceptance Model, and the Unified Theory of Acceptance and Use of Technology (UTAUT) are essentially psychological theories that seek to uncover a single truth by speculating and putting to the test the relationship between independent and dependent variables.

4.2 E-HRM adoption research framework

An essential framework for e-HRM adoption study has emerged from the comprehensive literature review. After reading all the research articles and summarising them, the analysis has found a number of key elements that affect the acceptance of e-HRM and the results (anticipated and real) of e-HRM implementation (Appendix 1). Based on the theoretical foundation and significant variables/constructs, the factors impacting e-HRM adoption have been compiled and organised.

4.4. Discussion

Identification of the factors influencing the adoption of e-HRM is the primary goal of the systematic literature review. The review produced a framework with four groups—system and technology, organisational, users/individuals, and environmental and contextual factors—that have an impact on the adoption of e-HRM. This e-HRM framework takes the stance that systems and technology by themselves are insufficient. There are more aspects that will impact the acceptance and adoption of e-HRM. We'll talk about any problems and opportunities in each factor below.

4.4.1 System and Technology Characteristics

System and technology place emphasis on the idea that technological traits can have an impact on how quickly an IS is adopted (Chakrabortya & Mansor, 2013). E-HRM, or electronic human resource management, is essentially a computerised system that supports information processes in human resources operations, such as selection and recruitment processes, training, or performance review. As a result, the technology and e-HRM system must guarantee the accuracy of the information that moves both inside and outside of businesses. E-HRM adoption is influenced by a variety of system and technology elements, according to this systematic research evaluation. External elements like the system and technology have an impact on our internal attitudes, beliefs, intentions, and behavior.

System and technology characteristics are theoretically underpinned by the technological acceptance model. According to the model, a user's attitude about his or her intention to use and actual usage of IS, as well as their feelings of favorability or unfavorability toward using the technology, are significantly influenced by the system's quality, perceived usability, and perceived utility.

Additionally, according to the signalling theory, a user's perception has a significant role in whether or not they embrace and use a technology. It invites the user to apply for a job that an organisation is offering (Kashi & Zheng, 2013). As a result, the e-HRM system must consider the potential impact of the website and its features, which could increase or decrease the adoption and acceptability of the IS, such as language standardising (Heikkila & Smale, 2011).

4.4.2 Organizational Characteristics

Organizational traits may have an impact on e-HRM adoption within an organisation. This thorough analysis of the literature reveals some crucial organisational traits. First, a high level of management commitment and senior management support can influence the extent of e-HRM adoption in a business (Troshani et al., 2011). Employee acceptance and adoption of e-HRM in firms can be influenced by management commitment and senior management support.

According to Panayotopoulou et al. (2010), organisational size and the degree of centralization are significant factors in the adoption of e-HRM.Because potential benefits can be shared among a large user base, organisations with big employee populations can use and embrace e-HRM to support their business processes, however it does have complexity issues. Additionally, the degree of centralization influences the adoption of e-HRM when choices are taken at higher levels of the organisational hierarchy, which eventually raises the level of e-HRM adoption.

Organizational status is a significant feature that may inspire potential candidates to apply for a job in the e-recruitment instance (Llorens, 2011). It is asserted that a company with a high organisational status will have more opportunities to maintain both the quality of the applicant pool and the general calibre of new personnel.

4.4.3 Users/Individuals Characteristics

The literature research identifies a variety of user and individual characteristics that affect the adoption of e-HRM. System and technological variables have to do with how well the users will be able to operate and utilise the systems and technologies. Because each user has a unique set of IT skills and knowledge as well as a unique background dealing with IT, their level of adoption will vary. The degree of e-HRM adoption at the individual level is found to be significantly influenced by the user's gender, age, application-specific efficacy, and educational level.

4.4.4 Environmental and Contextual Factors

Industry features and supporting infrastructure are examples of environmental and contextual elements that reflect the setting in which companies operate (Chakrabortya & Mansor, 2013). First, a significant aspect affecting the adoption of e-HRM is the extent of Internet penetration in the nation and society. It's because the Internet and its supporting infrastructure are necessary for the application of e-HRM technology. The adoption of e-recruitment is found to be significantly influenced by social and peer pressure, particularly users' intentions to use the system.

4.4.5 E-HRM Adoption and Outputs

The literature study focuses on a number of the previously mentioned elements that affect the adoption of e-HRM. Furthermore, a variety of conceptions have been utilised in various studies to quantify the adoption of e-HRM, according to the systematic literature review. Some research assesses the user's perception of the adoption of e-HRM. However, gauging a user's attitude alone is insufficient, hence some studies advocate using behavioural metrics including intention to use, usage behaviour, and actual system utilisation.

The literature evaluation also reveals the results of organisational and individual adoption of e-HRM. The e-HRM user will experience high system satisfaction on an individual level and low occupational stress, according to Wickramasinghe (2010). (Konradt et al., 2006). Additionally, the research on e-HRM adoption includes a number of indicators at the organisational level to gauge its effects. Because the employed e-HRM systems will transform and facilitate the role of HR, e-HRM adoption research evaluates the results by evaluating HRM effectiveness, effective communication, cost and efficiency, increase the value of HR, and business process improvement.

5. Conclusion, Implications & Limitations

Researchers have a few options to dig further into the adoption of e-HRM and so advance the theoretical and practical of e-HRM study. Almost 10 papers, to start, don't adequately describe the theoretical underpinnings of their study. The theoretical lenses to be used for empirical analysis in future research must be clearly determined and stated. In order to better comprehend how the e-HRM system will be embraced and accepted, it is also advised to use and integrate two separate ideas as the theoretical lenses. Second, the majority of e-HRM adoption used cross-sectional data rather than longitudinal data. In order to investigate before and after the adoption of e-HRM and to explain the actual results of e-HRM for HR practises and business processes within organizations, future research can make use of longitudinal data. Future empirical studies may also examine the mechanism behind e-HRM adoption and test the framework for adoption across various industries. Further research may shed more light on the nature and significance of the contextual factors that encourage or inhibit the adoption of e-HRM, even though many studies have focused on the technological determinism.

5.1 Managerial Implications

This work contributes to management and practise in addition to research and theoretical viewpoints. Most people typically think that implementing IS technology will have benefits, without paying much attention to other important considerations. Therefore, it is necessary to observe e-HRM activity from the system and technology, organisational, users'/individuals', and contextual/environmental perspectives in order to adopt a more holistic approach.

5.2 Limitations

The systematic literature review has significant drawbacks, even though it gives future research a direction. First off, the e-HRM framework's components and attributes have not been explicitly linked in this research's detailed assertions. In order to locate the pertinent papers, the researchers also searched two well-known databases. These databases might have also left out some pertinent research. However, the systematic review's meticulous process has decreased the likelihood of leaving out important papers. It is advised that future researchers immediately access pertinent papers from peer-reviewed journals. In order to progress both research and practice, this framework should offer a way to aid in the integration of the research in e-HRM studies.

REFERENCES

1. Chakrabortya, A. R., & Mansor, N. N. (2013). Adoption of human resource information system: a theoretical analysis. Procedia - Social and Behavioral Sciences, 75, 473-478. https://doi.org/10.1016/j.sbspro.2013.04.051
2. Crossan, M. M., & Apaydin, M. (2010). A multi-dimensional framework of organizational innovation: a systematic review of literature. Journal of Management Studies, 47(6), 1154-1191. https://doi.org/10.1111/j.1467-6486.2009.00880.x
3. Davis, D. F. (1989, September). Perceived usefulness, perceived ease of use and user acceptance of information technology. MIS Quarterly, 13(3), 319-340. https://doi.org/10.2307/249008
4. DeLone, W. H., & McLean, R. E. (1992). Information system success: the ques for the dependent variable. Information System Research, 3(1), 60-95. https://doi.org/10.1287/isre.3.1.60
5. Florkowski, G. W., & Olivas-Lujan, M. R. (2006). The diffusion of human-resource information-technology innovations in US and non-US firms. Personnel Review, 35(6), 684-710. https://doi.org/10.1108/00483480610702737
6. Harris, M. M., Hoye, G. v., & Lievens, F. (2003). Privacy and attitudes towards Internet-based selection systems: a cross-cultural comparison. International Journal of Selection and Assessment, 11(2-3), 230-236. https://doi.org/10.1111/1468-2389.00246

7. Heikkila, J.-P., & Smale, A. (2011). The effects of 'language standardization' on the acceptance and use of e-HRM systems in foreign subsidiaries. Journal of World Business, 46(3), 305-313. https://doi.org/10.1016/j.jwb.2010.07.004
8. Huang, J., & Martin-Taylor, M. (2013). Turnaround user acceptance in the context of HR self-service technology adoption: an action research approach. The International Journal of Human Resource Management, 24(3), 621-642. https://doi.org/10.1080/09585192.2012.677460
9. Kashi, K., & Zheng, C. (2013, March). Extending Technology Acceptance Model to the e-recruitment context in Iran. International Journal of Selection and Assessment, 21(1), 121-129. https://doi.org/10.1111/ijsa.12022
10. Keller, C. (2005). Virtual learning environments: three implementation perspective. Learning, Media and Technology, 30(3), 299-311. https://doi.org/10.1080/17439880500250527
11. Konradt, U., Christophersen, T., & Schaeffer-Kuelz, U. (2006). Predicting user satisfaction, strain and system usage of employee self-services. International Journal of Human-Computer Studies, 64(11), 1141-1153. https://doi.org/10.1016/j.ijhcs.2006.07.001
12. Lapointe, L., & Rivard, S. (2005). A multilevel model of resistance to information technology implementation. MIS Quarterly, 29(3), 461-491. https://doi.org/10.2307/25148692
13. Legris, P., Ingham, J., & Collerette, P. (2003). Why do people use information technology? a critical review of the technology acceptance model. Information and Management, 40(3), 191-204. https://doi.org/10.1016/S0378-7206(01)00143-4
14. Lin, H.-F. (2010). Applicability of the extended theory of planned behavior in predicting job seeker intentions to use jon-search websites. International Journal of Selection and Assessment, 18(1), 64-74. https://doi.org/10.1111/j.1468-2389.2010.00489.x
15. Lin, L.-H. (2011). Electronic human resource management and organizational innovation: the roles of information technology and virtual organizational structure. The International Journal of Human Resources Management, 22(2), 235-257. https://doi.org/10.1080/09585192.2011.540149
16. Lin, L.-H. (2011). Electronic human resource management and organizational innovation: the roles of information technology and virtual organizational structure. The International Journal of Human Resources Management, 22(2), 235-257. https://doi.org/10.1080/09585192.2011.540149
17. Marler, J. H., & Fisher, S. L. (2013). An evidence-based review of e-HRM and strategic human resources management. Human Resources Management Review, 23, 18-36. https://doi.org/10.1016/j.hrmr.2012.06.002
18. Martins, L. L., & Kellermanns, F. W. (2004). A model of business school students's acceptance model of a web-based course management system. Academy of Management Learning and Education, 3(1), 7–26. https://doi.org/10.5465/AMLE.2004.1243681
19. Mueller, D., & Strohmeier, S. (2011). Design characteristic of virtual learning environments: state of research. Computers and Education, 57, 2505-2516. https://doi.org/10.1016/j.compedu.2011.06.017
20. Ngai, E., & Wat, F. (2006). Human resource information systems: a review and empirical analysis. Personnel Review, 35(3), 297-314. https://doi.org/10.1108/00483480610656702
21. Panayotopoulou, L., Galanaki, E., & Papalexandris, N. (2010). Adoption of electronic system in HRM: is national background of the firm relevant? New Technology, Work and Employment, 25(3), 253-269. https://doi.org/10.1111/j.1468-005X.2010.00252.x
22. Panayotopoulou, L., Vakola, M., & Galanaki, E. (2007). e-HR adoption and the role of HRM: evidence from Greece. Personnel Review, 36(2), 277-294. https://doi.org/10.1108/00483480710726145
23. Parry, E. (2011). An examination of e-HRM as a means to increase the value of the HR function. The International Journal of Human Resource Management, 22(5), 1146-1162. https://doi.org/10.1080/09585192.2011.556791

24. Parry, E., & Tyson, S. (2011). Desired goals and actual outcomes of e-HRM. Human Resource Management Journal, 21(3), 335–354. https://doi.org/10.1111/j.1748-8583.2010.00149.x
25. Payne, S. C., Horner, M. T., Boswell, W. R., Schroeder, A. N., & Stine-Cheyne, K. J. (2009). Comparison of online and traditional performance appraisal systems. Journal of Managerial Psychology, 24(6), 526-544. https://doi.org/10.1108/02683940910974116
26. Rahim, M. M., & Singh, M. (2007). Understanding benefits and impediments of B2E e-business system adoption. Journal of Internet Commerce, 6(2), 3-17. https://doi.org/10.1300/J179v06n02_02
27. Ruta, C. D. (2005). The application of change management theory to HR portal implementation in subsidiaries of multinational corporations. Human Resource Management, 44(1), 35-53. https://doi.org/10.1002/hrm.20039

Appendix 1 E-HRM Adoption Research Framework

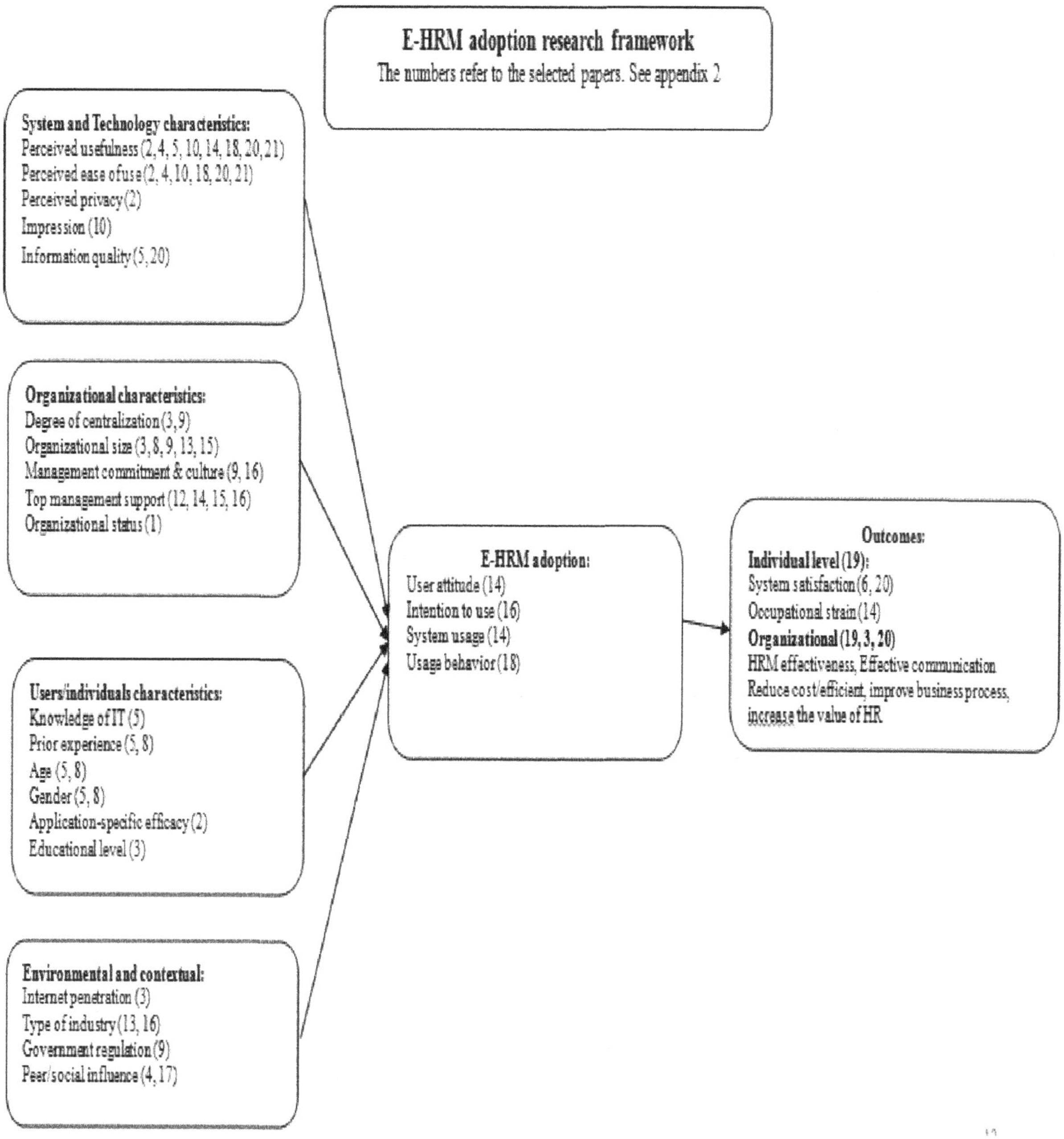

Appendix 2 List of the research papers

No	Authors	Research Questions/Research Problem	Variables/ andHypotheses	Theoretical Underpinning	Method	Findings
1	Llorens, 2011	Public sector E-recruitment adoption framework in the US	high-status andlow-status organizations and its impact on candidate pool quality and the overall quality of new hires	Windolf's typology framework for e-recruitment adoption	Survey	- e-recruitment technologies will hold the potential candidates - The role of third-party e-recruitment is important
2	Tong, 2009	The employed jobseekers' perceptions and behaviors of third-party e-recruitment technology adoption in Malaysia.	Perceived usefulness (PU), perceived ease of use (PEOU), behavioural intention (BI), perceived privacy risk (PPR), Performance	Technology Acceptance Model (TAM)	Survey	Perceived usefulness, perceived privacy risk, performance expectancy, application-specifi c self-efficacy affect employed
			expectancy (PE), Application specific self-efficacy (ASSE), Perceived stress (PS)			jobseekers' perceptions and behaviors
3	Panayotopoulou, Galanaki, & Papalexandris, 2010	how the national background affects the use of e-HRM	- Organizational level factors: size, firm performance, educational level of the members - HRM Context: centralization of HRM functions, strategic importance of HRM function, internal communication, training - National culture, internet penetration, economy	None specific	Mix between survey and secondary data Cluster analysis	socio-cult ural context, organizat ional context and HRM characteristics affect e-HRM adoption
4	Lin, 2010	Predicting job seeker intentions to use job-search websites	- Attitudinal belief structure: Perceived Usefulness, Perceived ease of use - Normative belief structure: Peer Influence, External Influence - Behavioral control belief structure: perceived behavioral control	Extended Theory of Planned Behavior		attitudinal, normative, and behavioral control beliefs influence user adoption intentions

5	Voermans & Veldhoven, 2007	attitude towards electronic human resource management (E-HRM)	IT experiences: ease of use, usability, output quality, user support Preferred HR role: employee champion, change agent, administrative expert, strategic partner Control variable: job experience, length of service, knowledge of IT, age, gender	Technology Acceptance Model (TAM)	Survey	Perceived usability is related to attitude towards e-HRM
6	Payne, Horner, Boswell, Schroeder, & Stine-Cheyne,	Compare employee reactions to the use of an online performance appraisal (PA) system	Rater accountability, Security of the ratings, Quality of the evaluation,	None specific	Survey	Employees rate with the online version reported significantly
	2009	to the traditional paper-and-pencil (P&P) approach	Satisfaction with the PA, Utility of the PA, Participation in the PA			higher levels of rater accountability and employee participation than employees rate with the traditional instrument
7	Panayotopoulou, Vakola, & Galanaki, 2007	the transformation in the role of the HR function in Greek firms, as a result of the use of internet and technology	-	None specific	qualitative and quantitative methodology, which involved focus groups and questionnaires	- E-HRM for facilitation of staffing procedure and communication. - e-HR adoption differs by sector type - Organization al culture, employee IT skills, collaboration of HRM and IT are the critical factor for adoption
8	Wickramasinghe, 2010	investigate employee perceptions towards web-based electronic HRM systems in Sri Lanka	Organizational characteristics: size, sector, age of e-HRM system System conditions and performance: time related, cost related, organizational performance Individual characteristics: age, gender, prior experience	None specific	Survey	The web-based HRM system acceptance is assessed based on the user satisfaction and system usage. It is influenced by organizational characteristics, system condition and individual characteristics

9	Troshani, Jerram, & Hill, 2011	The factors that influence the organizational adoption of HRIS in public sector organizations.	Environment context: Regulatory compliance, Successful adoptions Organizational context: Technology competency, Management commitment, size, centralization	None specific	qualitative exploratory	Environment context and organizational context have deep influenced the e-HRM adoption.
10	Kashi & Zheng, 2013	Factors influencing applicants' behavioral intentions to apply for jobs online	Perceived usefulness Perceived ease of use Behavioral intention Impression	Technology Acceptance Model (TAM) and signaling theory	Survey	Perceived usefulness, perceived ease of use behavioral intention impression are

DISCOVERING THE POTENTIAL OF ARTIFICIAL INTELLIGENCE FOR AUGMENTING EFFICIENCY IN AGRICULTURAL SECTOR

Shimna C U
Research Scholar, Department of Commerec & Management Studies, PSMO College, Tirurangadi
Mail id: iyashishu@gmail.com

Dr Ayoob C P
Research Supervisor, Department of Commerec & Management Studies, PSMO College, Tirurangadi
Mail id: ayoobkeyi@gmail.com

Abstract

Rising population and soaring food demand are the recent concerns straining agricultural sector. The sector is struggling with these bottlenecks being unable to meet the needs with its ongoing traditional systems which has made farming unprofitable and hence less attractive among people for livelihood Furtherance of agriculture with recent technologies of artificial intelligence is the need of the hour. Artificial Intelligence has already demonstrated its proficiency in all sectors including agriculture. Extensive adaption of artificial intelligence in agricultural sector might enable farmers to boost their productivity with limited resources. By using artificial intelligence in farming, farmers can access relevant information and numerous tools which would improve efficiency and production with minimal ecological blemishes. Application of AI in agriculture commences right from sowing through assistance to choose the right time and seed suiting the weather conditions till the marketing of produce with adequate price related information. In short, Artificial Intelligence is the panacea for the challenges such as crop diseases, improper storage management, lack of market information, weather related issues and so on the sector is confronting for years. This paper examines the applications of AI in the field of agriculture. The paper describes how efficiency of various processes in agriculture can be improved through Artificial Intelligence.

Keywords: *Artificial Intelligence, Agriculture, Farming, Information Technology, Internet of Things.*

1. Introduction

Agriculture is the primary and prominent sector which serves as the initial step towards the development of each nation. But recently, increasing demand for food arising out of population explosion is putting pressure on the sector. As per the estimates of FAO, world population will increase to two billion by 2050 whilst the cultivable land will be scaled down to 4%. In this scenario, food sufficiency can only be ensured by employing technological advancements in agriculture resolving the enduring trials and tribulations (Khandelwal & Chavhan, 2019). Agricultural sector faces a lot of bottlenecks from sowing to harvest such as climate changes, soil fertility issues, labour shortage, inadequate scientific storage, transportation problems, less access to information and so on. The sector is struggling with these bottlenecks being unable to meet the needs with its ongoing traditional systems which has made farming unprofitable and hence less attractive among people for livelihood. Although agricultural sector has adapted many technologies, extensive employment of Artificial Intelligence is necessary to achieve fulfilment of needs by resolving the challenges. The recent researches and advancements in Information and Communication Technology have identified the scope of Artificial Intelligence in recasting agricultural sector. Embracing suitable technologies in AI enables to carry out agricultural practices systematically with nominal human labour requirements. Digitalization of agriculture is gaining attention due to its capability to move towards the sustainable development goals with minimum resources and extravagance. Agriculture has already tasted the sweetness of mechanization which has actualized hours of efforts and tasks done all of a sudden. The main part of AI is machine learning which involves feeding the machine with statistical as well as past data on the basis of which the task is executed. Application of artificial intelligence and Internet of Things backed up with proficient decision making system can bring wonders in agricultural system with minimum human intervention. Artificial Intelligence and Internet of Things is considered as the two sides of a coin (Subeesh & Mehta, 2021). Dependency of farming practices upon the unpredictable environmental conditions like climate and weather augments farmers' troubles which can only be resolved through proper execution and employment of Artificial Intelligence Technologies. This study mainly deals with various applications of AI technologies in agriculture for smoothening the primary sector of the economy.

2. Need for Artificial Intelligence and automation in agriculture

Artificial intelligence (AI) is a field of computer science that uses, among other aspects, machine and deep learning algorithms to learn from and interpret data in order to resemble human intellect. Artificial Intelligence is a modern tool which involves development of computer systems, robotics and other digital equipments which is able to perform various tasks which requires human interventions. The AI-based approach provides a specific solution to a defined complicated problem rather than generalising the issue. Owing to their benefits over conventional systems, artificial neural networks have been used to the agriculture industry several times. By providing support in selecting appropriate crop kinds, implementing better soil and nutrient management methods, managing pests and diseases, calculating crop production and forecasting commodity prices, AI technology may help farmers to elevate yields. In order to solve problems in agricultural sector, AI employs deep learning, robotics, Internet of Things, image processing, artificial neural networks, wireless sensor networks (WSN), machine learning, and other cutting-edge techniques. Big data, AI, and Machine Learning technologies may be used to forecast prices, estimate quantity of output and yield, and spot pest and disease infestations. They may provide farmers with guidance on both supply and demand, the best crop kinds to plant for increasing productivity, the proper usage of pesticides, and anticipated price trends. AI technology is assisting people in various sectors to overcome the barriers arising out of traditional systems. AI provides required information to the farmers under various circumstances which enables farmers to think and take decisions appropriately (Smith, 2020).

3. Applications of Artificial Intelligence in Agriculture

3.1 Soil Management

Knowing the characteristics of soil and planning to cultivate accordingly is the first step in agriculture. Understanding the nature of soil and carrying out further activities enhances the productivity. Attributes of soil and fertility can be known with the help of artificial intelligence which enables the farmers to carry out activities to improve the condition of soil. AI applications like Management Oriented Modelling (MOM) reduces leaching of nitrate from soil and enhances production as it is capable of evaluating the alternatives based on users' requirements. The Artificial Neural Network (ANN) can predict soil texture, monthly mean temperature of soil and soil nutrients after erosion on the basis of characteristics observed from coarse resolution soil maps (Sarkar et al., 2018a).

3.2 Crop Management

Crop management involves a chain of activities to improve the growth and yield of the crop which starts with sowing and continues with regular observation, harvest, storage and distribution of the product. Precision crop management is a new concept which aims at managing the crops by understanding the requirements of a particular field and crop which would improve the productivity by ensuring sustainable growth. However, these technique hasn't yet adopted due to dearth of timely data regarding the state of soil and crops. CALEX technology assists farmers with guidelines for crop management and ANN technology helps to predict the crop yield, crop response to the changes in soil and helps to detect crop nutrition disorder. Another technology called Fuzzy Logic also enables proper crop management by reducing the pest attack over crops. Robotics is another AI technology which has proven useful for farmers in harvesting, which has eighty percent success rate, even though it is expensive and speed of harvesting is comparatively less (Clara Eli-Chukwu, 2019).

3.3 Disease Management

Agricultural sector is highly reactive to the changes in environment. One of such inelectable and uncertain risk which the producers have to deal with is disease management. Some diseases affected to the plants have the capability to destroy the total yield. So, taking care of the crops from disease affection and controlling the effect, once the disease has attacked the crops is necessary to minimize the loss. Adoption of integrated disease control management model might enable the farmers to control the effect of diseases, even though it is time consuming and costly. Web based Intelligent Disease Diagnosis System (WIDDS) accurately responds to the nature of disease affected. Another expert system using rule base helps in disease detection and ensures faster treatment at affordable costs. Fuzzy Xpest is another AI technology which imparts pest information to the farmers and enables disease forecasting. Compuetr vision system (CVS) and Genetic Algorithm are some other technologies which can be used in agriculture for disease detection (Clara Eli-Chukwu, 2019).

3.4 Weed Management

Weeds are another threat to the crops which reduces the yield downright. Researchers have reported that weeds are capable of reducing the yield up to 60%. The variation in the loss of yield from crops depends on crops exposure to weeds and its species (Rao et al., 2014). The destruction caused by weeds are not limited to abatement of yield but it has many other impacts like rampant fire, flooding, liver disease and allergic reactions, if consumed and so on. The growth of weeds are often controlled by using herbicides which has negative effects on both human health and environment as well (Sarkar et al., 2018b). The novel technologies in AI like UAV, Support Vector Machine (SVM) and ANN are capable of detecting weeds and other stress in crops which enables adoption of timely counter measures. This helps the farmers to remove harmful weeds without the usage of harmful herbicides through application of technologies like Sensor Machine Learning, ROBOTICS and Mechanical control of weeds. Another technology named Digital Image Analysis (DIA) has 60% success rate as per the reports of researchers which makes use of digital images taken by UAV (drone) (Clara Eli-Chukwu, 2019).

3.5 Yield Prediction

Yield prediction is another beneficial application of AI in agriculture which enables farmers to carry out further activities accordingly. Predicting the quantity of yield is very helpful to the farmers as they can adopt proper marketing strategies and estimate the cost in advance. Al technologies like Artificial Neural Network Model can predict yield on the basis of attributes of the soil by using back propogation learning algorithm (Liu et al., 2005).

3.6 Storage Management

Even thogh digitalization could intervene all the phases in farming, some activities like storage management remained as manual process. Storage of products always remained as a headache of the farmers since a small error can cause unmanageable loss to the yield. However, AI and IoT has recently brought new technologies to resolve these issues through proper storage monitoring. The quality of the produce under the storage can easily be monitored by employing Wireless sensor nodes. The cumulative numbers derived from the temperature and humidity sensors will help the farmers to understand the temperature and humidity variations in the storage units. Not just temperature and humidity levels, but application of MQ sensors helps to assess the level of carbon monoxide for better management. Application of CNN models can enable the farmers to detect pesticide residues on the crops so that it can be removed and cleaned to ensure food safety. Techniques like LDR sensors and smoke sensors can provide propr lighting and are capable of detecting the presence of fire in storage systems respectively (Jiang et al., 2019; Subeesh & Mehta, 2021).

4. Challenges in the application of AI in agriculture

Artificial intelligence has wider scope in agriculture as it is a solution for many problems encountered by agricultural sector since decades. Although, extensive adoption of AI for problem solving is risky as it poses many issues when it comes to practicability of these technologies. The first and foremost obstacle is lack of familiarity regarding these high tech machine learning techniques among the farming communities across the world. AI requires a lot of data to be feeded to the machines for accurate predictions which is difficult to obtain (Dharmaraj & Vijayanand, 2018). The data has to be filtered before uploading to the system as inputs, since the wrong inputs will produce wrong predictions and will result in worst performance. Almost all the AI technologies requires high speed internet connectivity and human expertize for constant monitoring at each stage. Another notable drawback of these technologies is its less reliabilty due lack of accuracy since the things like fluctuations in the weather are hardly predictable. The technologies like ANN and Fuzzy Logic which are meant for reducing pest attack in crops often fails to differentiate between crops and weeds (Yang et al., 2003). Usage of some of the heavy machines might also cause loss of fertility of the soil. The techniques such as ANN, DIA and CALEX are very time consuming and ROBOTICS, which can assist farmers in harvest consumes a lot of fuel (Clara Eli-Chukwu, 2019). All these drawbacks point out the difficulties in adopting AI techniques in agricultural sector. The decisions made using these techniques has direct impact on agriculture. Hence, the authorities should take all possible initiatives forthwith to enable extensive adoption of AI techniques as it is the pre-eminent solution for overcoming the challenges the sector is facing presently (Subeesh & Mehta, 2021).

5. Conclusion

It is evident that automation using AI and IoT techniques has key role in every face of farming. These techniques are capable of revolutionising agricultural sector and can make the farmers' life easier. The key areas of AI application in agriculture include soil management, crop management, disease management, weed management, yield prediction and storage management. In short, AI technologies are capable of providing creative and comprehensive solutions to most critical problems of agriculture. These technologies helps to identify the nature of soil which enables producers to choose suitable seeds and the fertilizer requirements of the soil which would enhance the productivity. The technologies like ANN, CALEX and Fuzzy Logic improves crop management practices through detection of nutrition disorder, dwindling pest attack and yield prediction. Disease detection and forecasting has also been made possible by AI enabled techniques for taking timely counter measures. UAV, SVM assists the farmers in detection of the presence of weeds and Sensor Machine Learning and ROBOTICS helps in the removal of destructive weeds without the usage of harmful herbicides. AI and IoT technologies even facilitates yield prediction which helps farmers for better marketing and cost estimation. Not just these, it is now proving its capabilities in post-harvest activities too as it has enabled storage monitoring and detection of temperature and humidity levels in the storage units. However, agricultural sector is still working with the traditional systems and manual labour since all these AI technologies haven't been extensively applied in the sector yet. The main reason for this is the challenges and hurdles in the implementation of these technologies among the farming communities who are less familiar with automation and these sophisticated technologies. Hence, Government should promote adoption of technologies and should educate the farmers regarding the working mechanism of these machines and techniques. The developers should keep the users in mind and should make it as viable as possible for better results.

REFERENCES

Clara Eli-Chukwu, N. (2019). Applications of Artificial Intelligence in Agriculture: A Review. *Technology & Applied Science Research, 9*(4), 4377–4383. www.etasr.com

Dharmaraj, V., & Vijayanand, C. (2018). Artificial Intelligence (AI) in Agriculture. *International Journal Of Current Microbiology and Applied Sciences, 7*(12), 2122–2128. https://doi.org/10.20546/ijcmas.2018.712.241

Jiang, B., He, J., Yang, S., Fu, H., Li, T., Song, H., & He, D. (2019). Fusion of machine vision technology and AlexNet-CNNs deep learning network for the detection of postharvest apple pesticide residues. *Artificial Intelligence in Agriculture, 1*. https://www.sciencedirect.com/science/article/pii/S2589721719300017

Khandelwal, P. M., & Chavhan, H. (2019). Artificial Intelligence in Agriculture: An Emerging Era of Research Article. *Researchgate*. https://www.researchgate.net/publication/335582861

Liu, G., Yang, X., & Li, M. (2005). An Artificial Neural Network Model for Crop Yield Responding to Soil Parameters. *International Symposium in Neural Networks*. https://doi.org/10.1155/2021/5584754

Rao, A. N., Wani, S. P., & Ladha, J. k. (2014). *Weed management research in India-an analysis of past and outlook for future*. http://oar.icrisat.org/8592/

Sarkar, U., Bannerjee, G., Das, S., & Ghosh, I. (2018a). Applications of artificial intelligence in agriculture: A review.*Pdfs.Semanticscholar.Org,7*(3). https://pdfs.semanticscholar.org/6e08/7108aa8048da8cfc82cdecb7071a55bab488.pdf

Sarkar, U., Bannerjee, G., Das, S., & Ghosh, I. (2018b). Artificial Intelligence in Agriculture: A Literature Survey. *International Journal of Scientific Research in Computer Science Applications and Management Studies*, 7(3). www.ijsrcsams.com

Smith, J. M. (2020). *Getting value from artificial intelligence in agriculture*. Animal Production Science. https://sci-hub.se/10.1071/AN18522

Subeesh, A., & Mehta, C. R. (2021). Automation and digitization of agriculture using artificial intelligence and internet of things. *Artificial Intelligence in Agriculture, 5*, 278–291. https://doi.org/10.1016/j.aiia.2021.11.004

Yang, C.-C., Prasher, S. O., Landry, J. A., & Ramaswamy, H. S. A. (2003). Development of a herbicide application map using artificial neural networks and fuzzy logic. *Agricultural Systems, 76*(2). https://www.sciencedirect.com/science/article/pii/S0308521X01001068

DOES THE PANDEMIC REALLY HIT AVIATION INDUSTRY? AN ANALYSIS

Shahana Karimbanakkal

Junior Research Fellow, Department of Commerce and Management Studies, PSMO College, Tirurangadi, affiliated to the University of Calicut, shahanakarimpanakkal@gmail.com, 9539049590

Munavver Azeem Mullappallykayamkulath

Assistant Professor & Research Supervisor, Department of Commerce and Management Studies, PSMO College, Tirurangadi, affiliated to the University of Calicut munavverazeem@gmail.com, 9048676459.

ABSTRACT

Aviation, one of the most global industries, fosters cross-continental connections by offering a rapid worldwide transportation network. It is an important enabler to achieve economic growth and development, facilitates integration into the global economy and provides vital connectivity on a national, regional, and international scale. India is one of the fastest growing aviation markets in the world. The covid 19 outbreak hit the Indian aviation industry very hard than any other industries in the globe. The industry faced the worst ever turbulence during Covid due to the travel restrictions. Majority of the airlines cut their operations drastically, the airports faced a massive reduction in their revenues. It was a trouble time to the aviation industry during pandemic due to the reduction of aircrafts by the airlines to sustain the cost, the downfall in the air passenger traffic and the block of fresh revenue etc., The study tries to probe the effect of pandemic outbreak on Indian aviation industry.

INTRODUCTION

The aviation business is extremely unstable and is adversely impacted by a variety of variables, including the pandemic breakouts. The aviation sector is likely one of those in every industry that has been struck the worst during the covid period (Suau-sanchez et al., 2020). Indian aviation is the fifth-largest in the world by number of passengers, with a domestic passenger count of 274.50 million out of a total of 341.05 million as of 2020 (IBEF, 2020). The airline industry, which relies heavily on people moving around, was one of the first to be severely impacted by the pandemic breakout in 2020 (Paliś Mariola,2021) Due to a nationwide lockdown and a total ban on commercial domestic flights from March 23, 2020, to May 25, 2020, the domestic aviation sector in India went through unheard-of difficult circumstances. According to the April–June (Quarter 1, Financial Year 2020) GDP data, India's overall GDP shrank by 23.9% year over year, with the travel industry suffering a decline of 47% (GDP DATA, 2020). According to the IATA, the COVID-19 crisis in the nation has worsened its effects in the Asia-Pacific region, and the pandemic may affect 29,32,900 jobs in the nation's aviation and related industry (IATA, 2020).

REVIEW OF LITERATURE

The aviation industry is likely one of the worst hit across all sectors (Suau-sanchez et al., 2020). (Srivastava, 2020) highlighted the potential impact of Novel Covid-19 on India's GDP and economy: Lockdown caused by COVID-19's eruption has had a significant negative impact on the aviation and tourism industries. (Chaudhary et al., 2020) examined the impact of COVID-19 on the Indian economy, and it was discovered that due to the pandemic, a high risk of a global recession due to the impending complete shutdown of all economic activities—production, consumption, and trade—to prevent the spread of COVID-19.

Most airlines had to come to a standstill as a result of the dramatic drop in passenger demand and country-specific flight bans; several businesses were forced to end practically all of their operations and ground entire fleets (Sun et al., 2020). Past severe failures, such as energy crises, financial crises, wars, and prior diseases, have not deterred the aviation sector, which has demonstrated its resilience (Bakır & Merkert, 2020).The airline sector is currently battling the epidemic while dealing with travel restrictions, landed planes, scheduling uncertainty, job losses, and a lack of current revenue (Ranganathan, Mohan et al. 2020). In 2020, according to data from the global aviation sector, airlines are predicted to lose $84.3 billion, representing a net profit margin of 20.1% (IATA, 2020). Airlines should seize cutting-edge digital opportunities throughout this extended period of recovery to ensure a smooth return of air transport and the innovative airline services have the potential to significantly impact consumer happiness and boost tourism (Ravishankar Balakrishnan, 2020)

IMPACT ON AIRPORTS

Airports play a crucial role in the economic prosperity of cities, nations, and regions and by serving airlines, moving people, and conveying cargo, they directly boost economies (IFC, 2020). The COVID 19 epidemic had a significant negative impact on airports by forcing their closure over safety concerns, which had a very negative financial impact. The AAI announced a 92% decrease in revenue from April through June 2019 to April through June 2020, from Rs. 2973 crore to Rs. 239 crores and from 14.5 million in January 2020 to 27,687 in April 2020, the decrease in passengers at AAI airports saw a significant drop (Pandey & Xalxo 2021). As a result of a drop in aviation traffic at several airports, AAI has experienced losses for the first time since its foundation. fiscal year 2021 saw a 65% drop in income from Rs. 12,837 crores to Rs. 4,482 crores, resulting in a loss of Rs. 2,814 crores as opposed to a profit of Rs. 1,985 crores (Chandra J,2021). The capacity of airports to collect revenue declined proportionately as air travel declined. With limited operational expense flexibility and set capital costs, this puts a significant strain on the airport's capacity to remain financially viable (Pandey & Xalxo 2021).

FLIGHTS AND PASSENGERS

From March 2020 onward, the COVID-19 pandemic had a significant negative influence on India's aviation industry; by March 23,2020 there were 433 confirmed cases, which was a rapid increase (Sidhu, 2020). As a result, the Indian government announced that domestic and international aviation travel will be prohibited beginning on March 24, 2020, and continuing indefinitely. It was crucial to limit citizen movement to the absolute minimum as India approached Stage 3, or communal transmission, of the pandemic (Sidhu, 2020). Following a two-month period of inactivity due to the national lockdown, airlines began to fly domestically again on May 25, 2020, operating on only one-third of their typical summer schedule and subject to a number of government limitations as depicted in the figure 1. The domestic flight operation restarted on May 2020 after the ban with 30,000 passengers. From the month of September 2020, the capacity for operating domestic flights increased from the limit of 45% to 60%. After the withdrawal of the ban and increased capacity for operating domestic flight, the air travel by the passengers showed a slow steady growth.

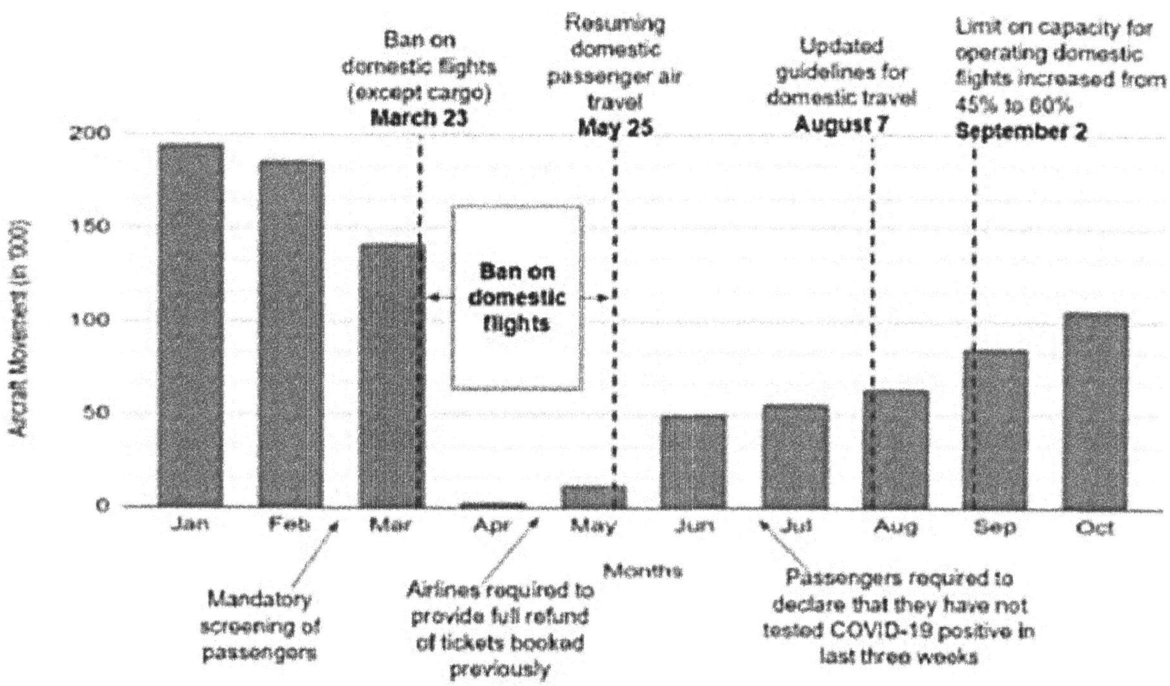

Figure 1: Government regulations and announcements related to air traffic control in India and the aircraft movement (Source: DGCA)

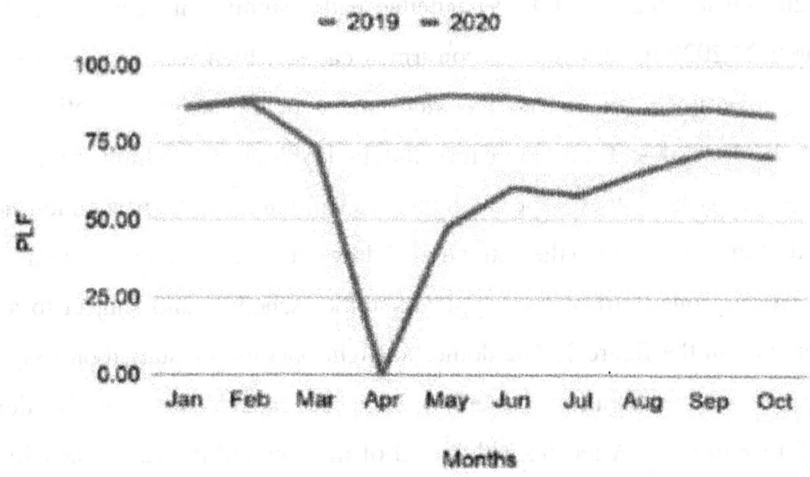

Figure 2: Monthly PLF for scheduled domestic aircraft movement in 2019 and 2020 considering SpiceJet, Vistara, IndiGo, AirAsia India, GoAir and Air India (Data Source: DGCA)

For the majority of domestic airlines, the PLF remained noticeably low. In figure 2, the total passenger load factor of six carriers are depicted. SpiceJet demonstrated a rapid recovery by exhibiting a load factor of 76% by August 2020; however, the other five of the six main Indian airlines under examination had a PLF in the range of 58% to 69% by that month (Sidhu, 2020).

CONCLUSION

Because of travel restrictions, a lack of leisure travel, and a lack of new revenue, the aviation industry has actually been among the worst affected. Due to this, the airlines were forced to reduce the number of aircraft, put personnel on unpaid leave, and turn to the markets for funding. The covid epidemic had a highly negative effect, and it struck the aviation industry particularly hard. Indian Airlines suffered a loss that was unprecedented. Due to a lack of sufficient revenue, the airlines restricted the number of aircrafts on the ground in order to cover costs. Both domestic and international passenger traffic are at their lowest levels ever. It was extremely difficult for the airlines to recover any kind of income and maintain their position in the market. Giving the grounded airlines a new lease of life in such a situation was difficult. In short the pandemic outbreak severely impacted the Indian domestic aviation industry which could stall development in emerging markets. It will be challenging to return to pre-Covid-19 2019 levels in terms of passenger numbers as the scenario is still evolving. It has previously been indicated that in order for the sector to recover, decision-making procedures would need to be modified, as well as new demands from the public will need to be met. If the pandemic stabilizes, the future will demonstrate which course businesses and industry will choose to recover in the most effective and efficient manner.

REFERENCE

Bakır, M., & Merkert, R. (2020). *Journal of Air Transport Management What can we learn from the JATM literature for the future of aviation post Covid-19 ? - A bibliometric and visualization analysis ☆. 89*(August). https://doi.org/10.1016/j.jairtraman.2020.101916

Chaudhary, M., Sodani, P. R., & Das, S. (2020). *Effect of COVID-19 on Economy in India : Some Reflections for Policy and Programme.* https://doi.org/10.1177/0972063420935541

IFC. (2020). *The Impact of COVID-19 on Airports : An Analysis.*

Potential impact of COVID-19 on the Indian economy. (2020). *April.*

Ravishankar Balakrishnan, C. B. P. (2020). EXPLORING THE FACTORS INFLUENCING AIRLINE CUSTOMER'S BUYBACK INTENTIONS FROM A TOURISM PERSPECTIVE. *PalArch's Journal of Archaeology of Egypt/Egyptology, 17*(9), 8399–8415.

Sidhu, P. K. (2020). *Impact of the COVID-19 Pandemic on the Indian Domestic Aviation Industry.*

Suau-sanchez, P., Voltes-dorta, A., & Cugueró-escofet, N. (2020). An early assessment of the impact of COVID-19 on air transport : Just another crisis or the end of aviation as we know it ? *Journal of Transport Geography, 86*(May), 102749. https://doi.org/10.1016/j.jtrangeo.2020.102749

Sun, X., Wandelt, S., & Zhang, A. (2020). Journal of Air Transport Management How did COVID-19 impact air transportation ? A first peek through the lens of complex networks. *Journal of Air Transport Management, 89*(May), 101928. https://doi.org/10.1016/j.jairtraman.2020.101928

CAPM, FAMA FRENCH THREE FACTOR MODEL AND FIVE FACTOR MODEL IN INDIAN STOCK MARKET: A CONCEPTUAL AND LITERATURESTUDY

Ms. Khadeeja

Farhana C P M

Research Scholar

Farook College (Autonomous)

Kozhikode E mail id:

khadeejafarhana12@gmail.com

Abstract

The performance of an asset pricing model can be adjudged in terms of how the model fairs in explaining the variations in returns of an underlying asset over time. This conceptual study reviews over the studies on CAPM, FF3FM and FF5FM and findings depicts that the performance of CAPM isinvalid and the individual performance of both three factor model and five factor model is better for explaining variation of stock returns in Indian context. Furthermore, size premium risk factors have more explanatory. In addition to this, the study reviews comparative study on these models to compare the ability of models in estimating stock return. The conceptual result indicates that the Fama French Five Factor Model outperforms than other model in describing the variation in expected stock return.

Keywords: *Capital asset pricing model, Fama French three factor model, Fama French five factor model, expected return, risk factor, Indian Stock market*

INTRODUCTION

The word "financial market" refers to any place where lenders and borrowers who have surplus and deficiency funds, respectively, come together to exchange instruments. Investors can take advantage of standard benefits if the asset is priced appropriately for them by taking into account all relevant elements that are affecting the value. If investors price the item correctly, taking into account all essential elements influencing the value, then they can enjoy typical profit by accurately pricing the asset in an efficient market. The rate of return and its determination are the most important concerns in finance. Higher risk has resulted in more profit, and vice versa. Investors should consider their risk- taking capability while deciding where and how to invest their money. During the early stages of the financial market, investment strategy was based on common sense, which measured overall risk and assumed that stocks with more risk yielded larger returns than lower risk ones. This basic framework contributed in the introduction of modern portfolio theories. The risk return tradeoff relationship is used to build single factor and multi factor asset pricing models. Using the asset pricing model, investors can calculate the degree of risk in their investments. Furthermore, the magnitudes of the expected return to be awarded for carrying any particular degree of risk can be measured. (Riyath, 2015).

In the beginning, 1960's, the single factor model also known as Capital Asset Pricing Model (CAPM) was developed of single factor known as beta. Arbitrage Price Theory (APT) suggested by Ross (1976) advocates that they are driven by multiple macroeconomic factors. Fama and French Three Factor model (FF3FM) in 1993 is the improved and extended version of the traditional CAPMas it is developing a multi-factor model with risk factors like in market beta, size of firm, book to market equity ratio (BE/ME) or Price-to-book ratio (P/B). Cahart four factor model is incorporating themomentum factor with FF3FM. (Riyath, 2015). Motivated by evidence and the valuation of 3F (Fama & French, 2015), have proposed a five-factor model by adding profitability and investment factors to the three-factor model. As depicted in figure 1, this study identifies three major areas (dark box) of namely; CAPM, Fama French Three Factor Model and Fama French Five Factor Model. Hence the main purpose of this paper is to conduct a conceptual review of the literature regarding above mention area in Indian stock market as these models have empirical evidence from international stock market and limited studies are a there in Indian stock exchange to predict expected return especially as a conceptual from comparative perspective.

Research Questions	**Objectives of the study**
How about the performance of CAPM, Fama French Three Factor Model (FF3FM) and Fama French Five Factor Model (FF5FM) and the explanatory power of risk factors in Indian Context?	To make conceptual analysis on the performance of CAPM, Fama French Three Factor Model and Fama French Five Factor Model and to know the explanatory power of risk factor in Indian context
Which asset pricing model Among this is better In Indian stock market?	To identify the better asset pricing Model among this in Indian stock market?

Data of this conceptual study is the review of CAPM, FF3FM and FF5FM and their comparative study in Indian stock market through the study carried out from 2001 to 2022 through Scopus database and Google Scholar.

Figure 1: An Evolution of Asset Pricing model

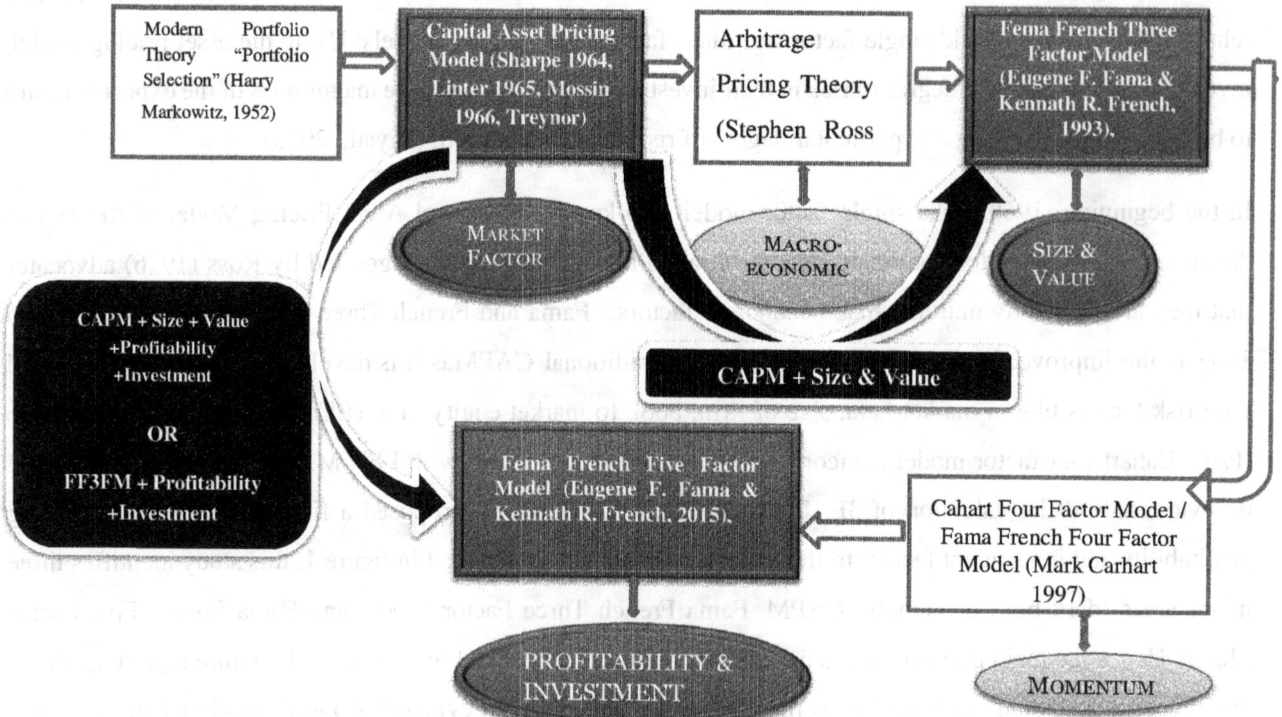

1. CAPITAL ASSET PRICING MODEL AND BETA IN INDIAN STOCK MARKET

(wijst, 2012)The CAPM implies that in equilibrium the expected excess return on any single risky asset is proportional to the expected excess return on the market portfolio. (Klockziem, 2018) CAPMassumes that the risk premium portion of a security's expected return is a function of that security's systematic risk, i.e. Beta.

$$Ri - Rf = Rf + \beta\,(Rm - Rf)$$

Ri = The asset i expected return or cost of capital Rf = The risk free rate β = The beta of asset
Rm = The expected return on the market

(Abhay Raj,Priya chocha,Nita lalakiya et al., 2017; Balakrishnan, 2016; Basu & Chawla, 2010; Chaudhary, 2016; Dhankar & Singh, 2005; jenet jyothi D souza, soumys shetty, 2019; Ratra, 2017) has tested the efficiency and validaty of CAPM either in BSE or NSE in Indian stock market and results indicates that the CAPM fails and have negative relationship between beta and excess return and indicating an inefficient capital market. The use of the CAPM model to choose the company's shares may result in wrong predictions to potential investors. The cause of inapplicability of CAPM is difference between expected and actual result is very high at normal risk level. CAPM does not have much explanatory power and recommended for search of alternative models for the asset price in India. Even though there is a weak correlation between realized excess return and expected return as per CAPM, Higher R square indicate that systematic factor have a significant contribution on stock returns and beta should be modified to better represent systemic factors. (Rabba, 2018) results explains that beta is unable the relationship between risk and return hence, CAPM is invalid.(Sreenu, 2018) to determine whether a higher risk is covered by a higher expected return and whether the connection between expected return and risk is linear, if beta is a complete measure of risk. The results indicate that the intercept is statistically insignificant.

- (jenet jyothi D souza and soumys shetty, 2019) examined CAPM in selected industries and except for Indusind Bank Ltd, Bajaj Finance Limited, Hindustan Unilever Ltd, Bajaj Auto Ltd, Hero Moto Corp Ltd, Maruti Suzuki India Ltd, Power Grid Corporation Of India Ltd, HCL Technologies Ltd, and TATA Consultancy Services Ltd, returns are not proportionate to beta coefficient in the most of portfolios. CAPM is valid in PSU, oil & gas, IT industry, Automobile and CAPM is invalid in Metal, FMCG and consumer goods industry in BSE (Singh, 2017).

1. FAMA FRENCH THREE FACTOR MODEL AND EXPLANATORY POWER OFSIZE & VALUE RISK FACTORS IN INDIAN STOCK MARKET

Following the development of the CAPM, academics raised concerns about the beta-returnrelationship and criticized the model as related only with the market portfolio. Fama and French (1993) developed a three factor model included two factors such as size and Book to Market equity (BE/ME) in addition to the market beta of CAPM as two factors were identified based on the study of Fama and French (1992). (Riyath, 2015)

$$Ri - Rf = Rf + \beta\,(Rm - Rf) + (SmB) + (HmL)$$

Ri = The asset i expected return Rf = The risk free rate β = The beta of asset Rm = The expected return on the market portfolio SmB is size premium HmL is Value premium

- *In case of Value effects*: (Harshita et al., 2015)(Manjunatha & Mallikarjunappa, 2018) (Sanjay & tripathi, 2007)Investigated the value effect and Alternative measures of value,such as book to market equity (BE/ME)and results reveal that Indian stock market shows a direct relationship between book-to-market equity ratio and returns. (Harshita et al., 2015), earnings to price (E/P), cash flows to price (C/P), and dividends to price (D/P), found statistically significant. The value effect is found to be significant on both an unadjusted and risk-adjusted return basis. A trading strategy based on the value effect has been shown to be economically viable.

- *In case of Size effects*:- (Sehgal & Tripathi, 2005) Using six different metrics of company size, including market capitalization, enterprise value, net fixed assets, net annual sales, total assets, and net working capital, researchers looked at the size effect and discovered a significant size premium. Moreover, the size-based investing strategy appears to be financially viable because it offers above-average returns on a risk-adjusted basis. (Mohanty, 2002) (Sobti, 2016)Once the size effect was taken into account, variables other than size had no additional explanatory power, despite the fact that size and price-to-book value were negatively correlated with stock returns.
- *In case of Value & Size effects*:- (Dash & Mahakud, 2014) implies that while the value impacts is frequently explained, the explanatory power of size effect remains consistent regardless of other asset pricing models risk adjustment process. (Mohanti & Jain, 2020) (Holani) Confirms the presence and significant effect of size and value effect in Indian stock market. (Balakrishnan, 2016) (Khudoykulov, 2020) finds that Size and value factors are still present in the Indian stock market and have been found to be successful investing techniques that optimize investors' wealth. When the size and value components are introduced to the CAPM, the ability to explain the variation in sample stock average returns is significantly improved. Most portfolios consider value factors to be significant. (Manjunatha & Mallikarjunappa, 2018) finds that Portfolio returns of small stocks are not explained by factorportfolios. For low BE/ME stocks, there is no need to derive size and value factors; market factor alone can explain the returns. However, size and value factors, in addition to market factors, are necessary for high and medium BE/ME portfolios.
- *Performance of FF3FM*:- (Gregory Connor, Sanjay Sehgal, 2001; Mohanti & Jain, 2020; (Manjunatha & Mallikarjunappa, 2018)Sehgal & Balakrishnan, 2013, (Durga, 2020)

(Holani)) finds that 3F model does a better job than CAPM by explaining the returns portfolios constructed based on company characteristics

2. FAMA FRENCH FIVE FACTOR MODEL AND EXPLANATORY POWER OF PROFITABILITY & INVESTMENT RISK FACTORS IN INDIAN STOCK MARKET

The evidence of certain studies says that FF3FM is an incomplete model for expected returnsbecause its 3 factors miss much of the variation in average returns related to profitability and investment through a five-factor model by adding these factors to the three-factor model. (Fama & French, 2015).

$$Ri - Rf = Rf + \beta\,(Rm - Rf) + (SmB) + (HmL) + (RMW) + (CMA)$$

Ri = The asset i expected return Rf = The risk free rate β = The beta of asset Rm = The expected return on the market portfolio SmB is size premium HmL is Value premium ***RMW*** is profitability premium CMA is Investment premium

- (Balakrishnan et al., 2018) (Raju, 2022) notice from the results that the average return patternclearly shows that the profitability & Investment factors have a significant impact on the Indian stock market. The results of asset pricing shows that the Fama-French five-factor model performs more credibly than the FFTF model in terms of accurately capturing portfolio average returns. (tripathi & pardeep, 2021) test applicability of FF5FM and results indicate that investment strategy based on profitability provide abnormal returns.(Foye, 2018) studies on Asia, Eastern Europe, Latin America an findings of Asia includes Indian stock market that FF5F no improvement and investment factor is redundant. Even though 5F model is poor, the study confirms the presence of investment and profitability factor. (Khudoykulov, 2020) Most portfolios consider investment factors to be significant.

3. COMPARATIVE STUDY OF CAPITAL ASSET PRICING MODEL, FAMA FRENCH THREE FACTOR MODEL AND FAMA FRENCH FIVE FACTOR MODEL IN INDIAN STOCK MARKET

- *Comparative study of performance of CAPM and FF3FM:-* (Lawrence et al., 2007; Sehgal & Balakrishnan, 2013; Sobti, 2016; Sreenu, 2018; Xiao, 2022) examined CAPM and 3F and results depicts that Fama-French Three-Factor model outperforms CAPM in explaining Indian stock market returns.
- *Comparative study of performance of CAPM, FF3FM and FF5FM:-* (Balakrishnan et al., 2018; Harshita et al., 2015; Khudoykulov, 2020) analysis suggests that the FF5FM performs admirably while the FF3F model maintains its capability to predict the average returns on portfolios. Moreover, (Lalwani & Chakraborty, 2019) implies that emerging market like India FF3F performs as good as FF5FM

FINDINGS, SUGGESTIONS AND CONCLUSION

The performance of an asset pricing model can be adjudged in terms of how the model fairs in explaining the variations in returns of an underlying asset over time. From the studies, it is identified that the performance of CAPM is invalid in Indian context. The individualperformance of both three factor model and five factor model is better in explaining the stock returns and the size risk factors contributes more explanatory power. Because when it comes to the value, it only contribute more explanatory power to high BE/ME portfolios. This study made an attempt to review the comparative study of these three models and in conclusion it finds that Fama French Five Factor model outperforms than other two models in Indian stock market.

Investors must recognize that many more factors must be examined throughout the stock selection process and the alternative versions of FF model are robust in explaining the returns on various characteristics sorted portfolios. Future research should focus on selecting the most appropriate asset pricing model to assess and forecast the expected return by enhancing the model and providing a substitute that truly takes into account the unique circumstances of the Indian capital market.

REFERENCES

Durga, D. (2020). Examining the validity of Fama French Three Factor Model in Indian Stock market -An empirical analysis. *international journal of management, II*(8).

Fama, E., & French, K. (2015). A Five factor asset pricing model. *Journal of financial Economics*, 1-22.

Holani, R. G. (n.d.). size and value related anomalies in indian stock market: empirical study using famafrench three factor model. *Vidyabharati International Interdisciplinary Research Journal.*

Klockziem, J. (2018). *Draft Capitalization Rate Study.*

N. S. Nanayakkara, P. D. (2019). Behavioural Asset Pricing: A Review. *International Journal ofEconomics and Financial issues, 2146-4138*, 101-108.

Rabba, D. (2018). An Analysis of CAPM in the Indian Equity Market.

Raju, R. (2022, March). Four and Five-Factor Models in the Indian Equities Market.Riyath, M. I. (2015). *An overview of Asset Pricing models.* GRIN.

Sanjay, s., & tripathi, v. (2007). Value Effect In Indian Stock Market.

tripathi, V., & pardeep, s. (2021). Fama French Five Factor Asset pricing Model: Empircial evidencefrom Indian Stock Market.

wijst, N. v. (2012). Capital asset pricing model and Arbitrage Pricing theory., (pp. 1-73).

Abhay Raj,Priya chocha,Nita lalakiya, Chocha, P., & Lalakiya, N. (2017). *Testing Capital Assets PricingModel as a Tool for Predicting Stock Returns: An Empirical Study in the Indian Context. 1*, 7.

Balakrishnan, A. (2016). Size, Value, and Momentum Effects in Stock Returns: Evidence from India. *Vision: The Journal of Business Perspective*, *20*(1), 1–8. https://doi.org/10.1177/0972262916628929

Balakrishnan, A., Maiti, M., & Panda, P. (2018). Test of Five-factor Asset Pricing Model in India. *Vision:The Journal of Business Perspective*, *22*(2), 153–162. https://doi.org/10.1177/0972262918766133

Basu, D., & Chawla, D. (2010). An Empirical Test of CAPM—The Case of Indian Stock Market. *GlobalBusiness Review*, *11*(2), 209–220. https://doi.org/10.1177/097215091001100206

Chaudhary, P. (2016). *Testing Of Capm In Indian Context. 37*(1), 18.

Dash, S. R., & Mahakud, J. (2014). Do Asset Pricing Models Explain Size, Value, Momentum and Liquidity Effects? The Case of an Emerging Stock Market. *Journal of Emerging Market Finance*, *13*(3), 217–251. https://doi.org/10.1177/0972652714550927

Dhankar, R. S., & Singh, R. (2005). Application of CAPM in the Indian Stock Market A Comprehensive Reassessment. *Asia Pacific Business Review*, *1*(2), 1–12. https://doi.org/10.1177/097324700500100202

Foye, J. (2018). A comprehensive test of the Fama-French five-factor model in emerging markets.

Emerging Markets Review, *37*, 199–222. https://doi.org/10.1016/j.ememar.2018.09.002 Gregory Connor, Sanjay

Sehgal. (2001). *Tests of the Fama and French Model in India*. 24.

Harshita, Singh, S., & Yadav, S. S. (2015). Indian Stock Market and the Asset Pricing Models. *Procedia Economics and Finance*, *30*, 294–304. https://doi.org/10.1016/S2212-5671(15)01297-6

jenet jyothi D souza an soumys shetty. (2019). An Empirical Examination of the CAPM on BSE SENSEX Stocks. *International Journal of Recent Technology and Engineering*, *8*(2S10), 678–685. https://doi.org/10.35940/ijrte.B1121.0982S1019

Khudoykulov, K. (2020). Asset-pricing models: A case of Indian capital market. *Cogent Economics &Finance*, *8*(1), 1832732. https://doi.org/10.1080/23322039.2020.1832732

Lalwani, V., & Chakraborty, M. (2019). Multi-factor asset pricing models in emerging and developedmarkets. *Managerial Finance*, *46*(3), 360–380. https://doi.org/10.1108/MF-12-2018-0607

Lawrence, E. R., Geppert, J., & Prakash, A. J. (2007). Asset pricing models: A comparison. *AppliedFinancial Economics*, *17*(11), 933–940. https://doi.org/10.1080/09603100600892863

Manjunatha, T., & Mallikarjunappa, T. (2018). Testing of Fama and French Factors in Indian CapitalMarket. *AIMS International Journal of Management*, *12*(1), 11. https://doi.org/10.26573/2018.12.1.2

Mohanti, D., & Jain, R. K. (2020). *Effect of Size and Value in Three Factor Model: Evidence from IndianEquity Market*. 8.

Mohanty, P. (2002). Evidence of Size Effect on Stock Returns in India. *Vikalpa: The Journal forDecision Makers*, *27*(3), 27–38. https://doi.org/10.1177/0256090920020304

Ratra, D. (2017). *Application of Capital Asset Pricing Model in Indian Stock Market*. 7.

Sehgal, S., & Balakrishnan, A. (2013). Robustness of Fama-French Three Factor Model: FurtherEvidence for Indian Stock Market. *Vision: The Journal of Business Perspective*, *17*(2), 119–127. https://doi.org/10.1177/0972262912483526

Sehgal, S., & Tripathi, V. (2005). Size Effect in Indian Stock Market: Some Empirical Evidence. *Vision:The Journal of Business Perspective*, *9*(4), 27–42. https://doi.org/10.1177/097226290500900403

Singh, A. (2017). Testing the Applicability of CAPM in Selected Indian Industries. *RamanujanInternational Journal of Business and Research*, *2*(1), 167–175. https://doi.org/10.51245/rijbr.v2i1.2017.126

Sobti, N. (2016). *Revisting Capm And Fama French Three Factor Model In Indian Equity Market*. *37*(1),16.

Sreenu, N. (2018). An Empirical Test of Capital Asset-pricing Model and Three-factor Model of Fama inIndian Stock Exchange. *Management and Labour Studies*, *43*(4), 294–307. https://doi.org/10.1177/0258042X18797770

Xiao, Y. (2022). *Comparison of the Applicability of CAPM and Fama-French Model in DifferentRegions:* 2022 7th International Conference on Financial Innovation and Economic Development(ICFIED 2022), Zhuhai, China. https://doi.org/10.2991/aebmr.k.220307.408

